"There are no shortcuts when it comes to relationships."

Anonymous

"Sometimes if you want to change things for the better, you have to take things into your own hands."

Clint Eastwood

"Every man should be embarrassed to die until he accomplishes something great in the world."

General Douglas MacArthur

"You seldom accomplish very much by yourself. You must get the assistance of others."

Henry J. Kaiser

"A true leader inspires others to lead themselves."

Ari D. Kaplan

"Average leaders lead followers, while great leaders lead leaders."

Anonymous

Building Relationships That Last a Lifetime
The NIA Way

Scott Talley

NIA Press
Houston, Texas

NIA Press, Houston, Texas

BUILDING RELATIONSHIPS THAT LAST A LIFETIME: THE NIA WAY.

Copyright ©2018 by Scott Talley

All rights reserved. No part of this book may be used or reproduced in any manner whatsoever without written permission from the author.

Printed in the United States of America.

Contributors: Stacy Harris and Moose Rosenfeld

Cover design by Danielo Rojas

Edited by Gwendolyn Weiler

ISBN-13: 978-0-69-205466-6

Dedication

This book is dedicated to my wonderful family. You all make everything worth fighting for. You have had to endure the struggles of entrepreneurship—the lows and highs of owning one's own business. To borrow an old phrase from my father, "Money is not everything, but it is way ahead of whatever is in second place!"

To my incredible wife, Moriah, you moved to this country from Mexico not knowing what the future would hold. You agreed to join me on this journey and have supported me through thick and thin. When times were most lean, you never complained. Your optimism in a brighter tomorrow is unwavering. I love you, and I'm so grateful you are in my life.

To my children, I could not be more proud of you. Danielle, you are my over-achiever who will go down in history as the greatest sister a sibling could ever want. When times are the toughest, you step up in ways that no sixteen-year-old should be expected to. Sofia, Alexa, and JeanCarlo, you bring so much joy to me with your laughter, singing, and incredible attitudes. I love you all dearly.

To my dad, John Talley, you exemplified hard work and preached constantly to your eight children that we could truly achieve whatever we set out to do. You taught us that the one way to make sure we succeeded was to put our heads down and go to work.

To my mom, Shirley, you taught us compassion for those less fortunate and that our efforts to help others should always be our highest priority. It gives me immense satisfaction to think about how over the coming years, thousands of those enrolled in our Network In Action groups will make real differences in their communities. This is a tribute to you and your gift in teaching us all that there is no higher calling than to serve others.

And finally, to God, who has blessed us with this incredible idea and opportunity to build real, lasting relationships with franchise owners and members of Network In Action. Together, we are making a real difference in the lives of business owners, and in the communities we reside in.

Now, on with the journey!

A Fitting Tribute

There are a number of times in the following pages where we reference a company called BNI®. For those of you not familiar with BNI®, the acronym stands for Business Network International, which was founded by Dr. Ivan Misner in 1985. Today, BNI® is the world's largest business networking organization and states that it now has over eight thousand chapters throughout the world. Dr. Misner is a New York Times Bestselling author who has written twenty-one books and created an entire industry around networking. He is often called the "Father of Modern Networking" and has been named by Forbes as one of the "Top Networking Experts to Watch."

Like many great visionaries, Dr. Misner obviously saw a need—in this case, the concept of business networking—and turned it into his personal empire. I cannot even imagine the number of business owners and the incredible number of hours that are donated each year to make all this happen for him. Building a worldwide company on the backs of volunteers and convincing so many to give so much for so long may very well be his greatest accomplishment! This book or its contents should in no way diminish BNI®. In fact, I personally owe a great deal of gratitude to Dr. Misner, as without his organization the inspiration for Network In Action simply would not have been there.

There are literally dozens of what I refer to as BNI® knockoffs in many parts of the world. What I mean by BNI® knockoffs is that people are stealing his ideas and methodologies to try and create competition in the marketplace. Many of these founders are motivated by anger at the way they may have been treated at BNI® or simply because they weren't allowed in the marketplace because that BNI® region was spoken for.

However, when I started Network In Action, I chose to make everything we do and the way we do it completely different. We were ridiculed and mocked by BNI® members who thought we had lost our marbles for entering this business networking space that had one dominant player—like an online store taking on Amazon!

Today, I can safely say that there is ample evidence that the NIA® way works! We do not require members to sign non-competes, we do not tell business owners they can only network in one place, and we do not require business owners to recruit members. Our leadership does not change every twelve months, and we save business owners over one hundred hours annually. At NIA® we do not have chairs, dances, and chapters! More important, every member is treated with respect and appreciation. And most important, every single NIA® group commits to give back annually by hosting a community project. At NIA® we will never rest on our laurels or assume that you do not have a choice when it comes to your marketing dollars, and that is just one of the many reasons we guarantee every members' investment in us!

Regardless of the frequent complaints and frustrations against BNI® that I encounter each day, I believe that Dr. Misner and I began with the same vision in mind, which is to create an opportunity for business owners to grow their businesses through networking and relationships. I honor his contribution to the marketplace and thank him for the foundation we are now building on.

Table of Contents

Preface 1

1 A History of NIA 1

2 You MUST Compare Apples to Oranges 8

3 Member-Centered Everything 14

4 Guaranteed ROI 20

5 Professional Community Builders vs. Volunteers 31

6 Meet Our Leaders 38

7 Ongoing Coaching 47

8 Monthly Meetings 52

9 Technology 59

10 Refer With Confidence 66

11 Building Your Community Through Service 71

12 Be a Value Creator 78

13 Networking Dos and Don'ts 84

14 To the Millennials 90

Preface

In the pages ahead, I will share what I believe will revolutionize the way businesses network across the country and the world. The concepts presented here are not theories, but are already changing the way business owners are networking today at Network In Action (NIA®) groups across the country. We have experienced so much in the last three years, and expect to experience so much more in the months ahead.

This revolution was inspired by three simple facts:

One, traditional networking groups today are run by volunteers who focus on guests rather than members. This wastes a tremendous amount of time—one of the few things we cannot replace.

Two, if properly led, a group meeting once a month can accomplish as much as, or more than, networking groups that meet weekly.

Three, we can stay connected when we are not meeting by utilizing today's technology.

I decided things could no longer remain as they were, and if we were to move forward, we had to assault the status quo. As you read, I offer this caveat from Mao Zedong, "A revolution is not a dinner party!" Noel Trichy wrote, "In a broad sense, what leaders do is stage a revolution." Webster defines the word revolution as, "An activity or moment designed to affect a fundamental change."

The question for you is: are you willing to look at a fresh and new perspective on an old networking model? Luckily, we are finding thousands of you out there who have been looking for a better mouse trap. Our tiny fire has quickly kindled into a bonfire. The revolution to change the way networking is done has only just begun. Our explosive growth will not be tackled alone, but we will do so with quality community leaders serving as our franchise owners, and quality members like you.

Life is about relationships. Many things in business are critical, but what matters most is really the relationships that you build and maintain with others, and the positive things you offer in the end. At NIA®, we have chosen to be about quality. We don't equivocate or shy away from that. Our goal is to bring on quality franchise owners and members who are people of integrity in their communities who understand that by bringing individuals together with the common purpose of helping each other, we all benefit.

When writing a book such as this, authors run the risk of appearing as if we think we know everything about a particular subject—in this case, networking. Before you jump to any conclusions, rest assured that this is not the case. I am so grateful to the many people over the years who have made an impression on my life. I have gained such an amazing perspective from so many at every turn.

As you read the pages ahead, our hope is that you will see the benefit of setting aside the Kool-Aid you've been drinking and join us as we take the networking industry by storm and revolutionize the way that things are being done. In return, our commitment to you—my commitment to you—is that we will always value your time, respect your ideas, and honor your commitment to helping all of us by "building relationships that last a lifetime."

1
A History of NIA

In 2014, I'd been working in the marketing industry for over twenty-five years. At the time, I owned a number of magazines and a large company with employees in thirty-seven states and two providences in Canada. We specialized in helping businesses increase their visibility by advertising with printed Yellow Pages and using that listing to connect with the Better Business Bureau and Chambers of Commerce. I was making more money than I had ever made in my life. I was driving a fancy sports car to a plush office every day, where I met with over a hundred sales representatives to pump them up for the day ahead. On paper and in person, I looked like success.

However, this was far from the case. So, this was the year that things would change.

I was starting to feel disconnected with the nature of my work. I grew up in one of those big, dysfunctional, Catholic families that seemed to function just fine, and I had come to realize I'm a hugger and a lover of people. I love connection! What I was doing professionally day in and day out didn't resonate with me. It didn't allow me to form deep relationships. I was in the business of transactions—not people. I met you, I sold you something, and when I came back a year later, you knew I was coming for money. During the entire fifteen years I was in business, I never had someone say, "Hey you have to call Scott to get a Yellow Page ad!" When I ran into clients at the store or in passing, they didn't flag me down to update me on their family or tell me about how their business was doing. There were zero relationships beyond the business transactions.

It wasn't that I was doing anything wrong. In fact, I wasn't just doing things by the book—I was doing things by *many* books. There are hundreds of books in publication about sales, increasing revenues, marketing, and retention. I have read the best of the best. I knew how to go in and get a sale. I knew how to leave with a check in my hand the majority of the time. I knew how to build an empire. Not only that, but I went to work every day and trained hundreds of people across the United States to do these things, and to do them well. By all measures, I was doing a great job: our customers list was growing, and our clients were very satisfied with the services we offered.

But I still had nothing in the way of meaningful relationships.

Let the Search Begin

About this time, my wife, Moriah, had gotten her real estate license. I was trying to find a BNI® group for her to join, but it was no small feat, as that residential realtor slot is usually the first one filled and the last one given up. I called the woman who runs the BNI® groups here in Houston, and she said there was a new group forming with an open spot for a realtor. It was our lucky day! Or was it? The group was meeting in Magnolia, Texas, which is a seventy-five-minute drive from our home in Houston. My wife would have to wake up at 4:30 a.m. every Tuesday morning to make it there by 7 a.m. If she missed the meeting or was late more than a couple times per year, she would be kicked out. If you know Moriah, you know this was not going to work for her, just as it would not for many others. It was not the perfect fit we were hoping for.

We kept doing our research, and, like many others around the country, we were offered the opportunity to start our *own* BNI® group closer to home. I thought that would be perfect, and I knew plenty of people who I could talk to about joining. We were excited as we thought about the benefits that would come from managing our own network of entrepreneurs investing hundreds of dollars into membership fees and meeting places each year. Surely there was some money to be made.

"How much does it pay?" I asked.

"It doesn't. It's a volunteer position. But your dues are comped!"

This response didn't exactly have me doing the happy dance the BNI® franchise owner was hoping for. In fact, it was quite the opposite.

"So, let me get this straight. I will build a group of twenty-plus individuals, manage the weekly meeting (held at the crack of dawn, no less), handle the books, monitor how we handle guest attendance, and work to keep our slots full in order to maintain the value of the group...to be compensated a grand total of $450 per year?"

This would be a good time to mention that I didn't even *like* networking at the time. I hated it. In fact, one night there was a networking event being held just across the street from our house in Memorial Park. It was half a block down from us. I walked there, and then I was back home within ten minutes. My wife looked at me in confusion. "What's wrong? Did you go on the wrong night?" she asked.

"No," I said. "I looked in the door at everything that was going on, and I just couldn't stand the thought of going inside. I'd rather stick bamboo up my fingers."

As I continued to discuss my disdain for networking with my wife, her bewilderment grew. "How can you hate networking when you love people and love helping them even more?" she asked. However, networking the way I had learned to do it, and the way that it seemed to be done everywhere I went, never seemed to be about people as much as it was about numbers. Ironically, it was *because* I love people that I hated networking so much.

So, yes, it was going to take a lot more than some comped dues to get me excited about getting up before sun up once a week to go do something I didn't want to do anyway. Needless to say, I did not go on to lead that group.

So, now what? Where was my wife going to network? How was she going to find a network that fit her lifestyle, instead of the other way around? We'd exhausted all our options and here we were without a solution. There wasn't a networking option out there that seemed to value people's time and offer any hope of creating real relationships among members.

At least, not yet.

An Idea is Born

That night, I was sitting in our living room, and I kept thinking to myself, *There has* got *to be a better way to do this.* The more I thought about it, the more I realized I did not hate networking. I hated the way it was being offered.

I grabbed my iPad and did a Google search for "reviews of networking groups." Five hours later, I crawled into bed at 3 a.m., but sleep was the furthest thing from my mind. My wife turned over and asked, "What in the world have you been doing?"

"Honey, I just came up with the best idea I've ever had."

When I started reading all of those reviews, I was seeing the same things over and over again. I grabbed a pad of paper and started writing down all the recurring themes. I saw that thousands of people don't want to—or *can't*—attend the morning networking meetings. No one enjoys the rollercoaster dynamic of being part of a group run by volunteers. People were fed up with the absence of technology in the industry. There were many stories of members referring other members only to find out that someone they referred had a criminal background. The fact that someone could write a check was enough for that person to get into the group! Countless people complained that they just didn't get any value out of the groups simply because of a number of items typically having to do with their basic structure and management.

In all of this, I saw that I wasn't alone. There were thousands of people expressing the same concerns, frustrations, and complaints with the current popular networking business model. Even more important, I saw that there was an entire community of people who were looking for their tribe.

That night, I created Network In Action.

I scoured the reviews, looking for the commonalities and the most pressing pain points. I was determined to create a group that would solve all of the most relevant issues and use that innovation to create more value for my group members. I was on a mission to change the networking industry. And I still am!

My vision is to revolutionize networking groups in much the same way Airbnb has affected the hotel industry and Uber has changed public transportation. Those businesses filled the demand for services that catered to consumers' lifestyles.

My right-hand man, Danielo Rojas, was ready for the challenge ahead. We went to work creating the technology we needed to create the most efficient networking opportunity offered on the planet. I would often wake up in the middle of the night with an idea and call him. The next day, he would give me a timeframe for accomplishing the task. Every idea was aimed at designing a model that would allow a monthly face-to-face group meeting to deliver the same value, if not more, as requiring a weekly meeting. We worked tirelessly on the technology resources for eight full months before we sold our first member.

Now, we have thirty-five groups and hundreds of members across the country—with new businesses and franchisees joining every week as we continue to steadily spread our influence across the United States. This is all in less than two years' time! People are coming, and they aren't leaving. Our retention rates are high, as members enjoy the value of our membership, their ROI, and the relationships they are forging. We are seeing so much success because people are hungry for efficient networking opportunities where the focus is on you, the member, instead of guests and prospective members. NIA® is specifically customized to fit into *your* lifestyle and to meet *your* networking goals.

The mission of NIA® is simple: It's our goal to put action into every networking meeting.

We satisfy that mission by setting ourselves apart in seven unique areas, which we will discuss in detail in the following chapters:

1. You are guaranteed a return on your investment, and we personally coach you how to get it.

2. Trained professionals run each group instead of a volunteer. This also happens to be their job, so you know they are going to be invested in getting you a positive return on your investment.

3. Monthly coaching sessions are included in your membership.

4. A monthly meeting instead of a weekly meeting, which saves you over eighty hours per year.

5. Technology: We actually have it, and it works from your smart phone to allow you to instantly connect with members when it's time to pass a referral—and to stay connected at all times. Our technology does not stop with an app, either. We will cover the amazing things we utilize in *Chapter 9: Technology*.

6. The NIA® marketplace offers members a place where you can offer your unique promotions to all of our members across the country.

7. Each member completes a background check and a personality profile so that you can refer to your personal network of friends, family members, and colleagues with confidence.

It goes without saying that I no longer hate networking. Now that I've found my tribe and created my niche, I love it! Today, I am officially out of the business of transactions, and I'm in the business of people. Now, I'm guaranteed to bump into you, as I get the pleasure of seeing my customers every month to get an update on their family and business ventures. I not only anticipate hearing about how their businesses are doing, but I am actively looking for people and resources who will help them grow. I get calls multiple times per week where someone is on the other end saying, "Hey, So-and-so told me I had to call you and get involved in what you have to offer. Where do I sign up?"

Many of those who have joined NIA® have become my closest friends. During my last birthday celebration, we held a party at the house, and I sat there at the end of the night looking around at the room full of people. The room was filled with NIA® members—customers who had become friends as we developed close personal relationships as a result of the NIA® business model. I smiled as I looked around, wondering who in the world my wife and I had hung out with prior to NIA®!

My heart was full as I looked at all those faces and thought about how we are all invested in helping each other's businesses grow. I thought about how that moment—so full of happiness and enthusiasm—was all made possible because I started taking notes on a legal pad one winter night.

I hope that as you read further, you too will consider joining our revolution.

2
You *MUST* Compare Apples to Oranges

When you recognize that networking is a powerful way to grow your business, it only makes sense to then ask, "Where's the most efficient place to network?" You want to focus your efforts and resources on the groups that are going to bring you the greatest return on your membership fee and, even more important, on the time you will be required to invest. Otherwise, your efforts are more like hunting big game with buckshot, and instead of producing results and growing your business, you are just being robbed of your valuable time and resources that would be better spent investing into your business.

When it comes to growing your business through networking, the adage *You can't compare apples to oranges* simply does not apply. In fact, in order to get the most benefit for your business, it behooves you to make that comparison. Up to this point, there have really only been two options out there for business owners who want to grow their businesses through networking: Weekly networking meetings run by volunteers with meetings focused exclusively on impressing guests, or Chambers of Commerce run by non-profits.

Historically, those who value networking have had to settle for joining one of these groups in an attempt to grow their businesses, only to come face-to-face with the reality that these are broken models that don't deliver as advertised. That's the boat I was in, which is why I was so disenchanted with the whole idea of business networking in the first place. Although both options may include some networking, that is where all similarities to Network In Action end.

Just as apples and oranges are both fruit but could not be more different, so it is with NIA® and the rest of the networking options.

And that is totally by design. I set out with the explicit purpose of being the exact opposite of what is currently being offered. I set out to be what a networking meeting *should* be—a time to network. Everything else out there dilutes that goal with group politics, cliques, members with ulterior motives, and basically a very flawed system.

Chambers of Commerce

I used to work with thirty-seven different Chambers of Commerce and Better Business Bureaus across the country, and I got to know them very well. Chambers are non-profits that have one focus and one alone, which is to help grow the economy in a particular city or in a particular area of the city. In order to do that, they want to attract more big businesses to the area. They want universities and large corporations to set up shop, which brings jobs and millions of dollars in annual revenues. That's who they want. But in order to fund that effort, they prop themselves up on the shoulders of *small* businesses like yours. They get a bunch of small businesses to pay $300-$400 a year with the perceived value being: *If I join this organization, I'll network and grow my business.*

Joining a Chamber can be a positive if you want to support your community. It can even be a positive if you are prepared to spend a huge commitment of your time attending ribbon cuttings and as many Chamber events as possible—making sure that you're the person who's there more often than your competition. Just keep in mind that Chambers love your competitors' dues as much as they love yours. That means that while

> **"I cannot even count how much money I have made"**
>
> *NIA® is the best business decision I have ever made. I was one of the first to join, and I am now going into my third year. I cannot even count how much money I have made off the group. More important are the trusted friends I have made. Today, I am surrounded by business owners who share the same challenges, and with NIA®, I am a phone call away from help. The model may seem new, but I strongly endorse it because it works!*
>
> **Rob Eppolito**
> **Video Mojo**
> **NIA® Heights Group**

Building Relationships That Last a Lifetime

you're going to be showing up with business cards in hand, ready to work the room, you'll be dodging a number of people in your very own industry. When you go to an event, you're going to be standing in a room full of multiple insurance people, numerous realtors, and a sea of people in your industry who recognize that if they attend more than you do, they're going to get the business. It's a game of survival.

So, how do you survive? Well, it's on you to figure that out. The Chamber isn't going to give you a handbook or a mentor to walk you through it. Come swim, sink ...or drown! It's all the same once your check clears. Outside of your ability to afford a few hundred bucks, the organization has no interest in you or the success of your business. The Chamber will do just enough to get you to renew next year. If you're not a great networker, or if you can't make it to the meetings and events frequently enough, then you're not going to derive any benefit from your membership. It simply becomes just another listing in another business directory.

That's very different from the NIA® experience. Here, you and your family matter, and your membership comes with ample coaching.

You may be able to glean a positive experience from your Chamber membership if you're an accomplished networker who is outgoing and gregarious. But make no mistake, *it is not a networking group*.

Let's face it—the entire function of the Chamber is not to help you network. It is exclusively meant to help grow that particular area in the city and to grow that particular area of the city. Most people go to these meetings to sell something, where in a networking organization like ours, you're there to build a relationship. You don't walk in the door thinking, *What am I going to get out of this?* You walk in the door thinking, *I'm here to take advantage of this*

> **"This is a classy organization that does everything right"**
>
> *One of the real benefits of NIA® is learning how to network. This is a classy organization that does everything right.*
>
> **Fabiana Cuggionni**
> **N2 Publishing**
> **NIA® West University**

opportunity to build relationships, and I need to spend this ninety minutes seeing who I can make friends with and who I can help.

Weekly Networking Groups: The Bad Apples

When it comes to networking, there are numerous models offered across the country with various acronyms in front of the group names. Almost all of them offer a singular model. They are almost identical in the prices they charge, the weekly meetings held at the break of dawn, the volunteer effort running the group, very little training for the next man up, and meetings built around impressing the guests instead of serving the members (all of which contribute to the networking roller coaster we will discuss in *Chapter 5: Professional Community Builders vs. Volunteers*). They have little to no technology, and anyone can join the group as long as they can write a check—no background checks required. The industry leader, BNI®, has been known to even require non-competes for volunteer leaders, and they either frown on your involvement in other networking groups or flat out forbid you to grow your business through business relationships outside their group.

BNI® is known for their "Givers Gain" mantra and philosophy. But let's take a minute to look at that. Can any business owner really get all the business they need from a single networking group? Of course not! I do not believe there is a business out there that has ever gotten all the business it needs from just one networking group—not even NIA®. We all still promote our businesses on the Internet, attend Chamber events, and spend our hard-earned dollars on marketing to keep our brand front and center. Yet, BNI® requires you to only participate in

> **"The reason I came over to NIA® is it's just a different model"**
>
> *I moved over from a well-known networking group I was part of for twelve years. The reason I came over to NIA® is it's just a different model. It's a higher dollar-per-capital of networking. The members are high caliber, and I look forward to helping the group with some quality referrals.*
>
> **John Schlacter**
> **TRW Commercial Real Estate**
> **NIA® Galleria Group**

one industry exclusive networking group in order for you to be a member of its group. Many business owners have been booted out or denied admission when they are honest about their participation in other networking efforts! In Katy, Texas, BNI® membership committees were specifically told not to admit anyone who mentioned on their applications that they are NIA® group members.

Can you imagine Uber telling you that you will be prohibited from using its services ever again if you dare to catch a Yellow Cab? Or Airbnb refusing customers who ever stay in hotels? This antiquated commandment from BNI® is a territory grab and nothing else. It is a fear-based decision meant to serve BNI® and BNI® alone—*not* the members who are paying dues.

However, this exclusivity comes with a double standard. BNI® has a "BNI® Ambassador" position, which is a political way to give privileges to certain members they value above others. Those in the ambassador positions are required to visit multiple groups a month to keep their ambassador status, but the payout is that they are able to grow their business by representing their brand in multiple groups—all while speaking out of the other side of their mouths and telling Joe Blow that he can only attend one group and just that one group in all the world. Is that consistent with "Givers Gain"?

> **"NIA® is for professionals interested in networking"**
>
> *Network In Action is for experienced professionals interested in networking. The majority of members are business owners with years of experience. I appreciate my group leader, Moose Rosenfield, for his hands-on involvement in vetting potential members to ensure he is bringing in great referral partners.*
>
> **Paula Marion**
> **Simple Operational Solutions**
> **NIA® Bellaire Group**

Today, NIA® groups are largely made up of former BNI® presidents, vice presidents, membership committee members, and ambassadors who all clearly see the hypocrisy of BNI®'s ways.

At NIA®, we believe that the more networking you do outside of our group, the more value you bring *into* our group. If your network is continuously expanding, then your ability to bring referrals to your fellow group members is continuously expanding as well. We are comprised of business owners who see the value in what NIA® offers and who appreciate the way we are truly committed to their growth and the growth of their businesses.

In the following chapters, we are going to give a thorough overview of the many ways that we have set ourselves apart from what is currently being offered. We are pioneering a new way of networking by moving forward with a new and improved model and actually focusing on what you came to do—which is to build your business through networking.

AT NIA WE DO NOT

Meet weekly

Allow transient volunteer leaders

Rely on outdated methodologies to pass referrals

Allow anyone to join

Meetings are not focused on guest

AT NIA WE DO

Meet monthly

Have professionals running the groups

State of the art technology

Require background checks

3
Member-Centered Everything

When I arrived at my first Network In Action meeting, I was instantly blown away. The energy, the people, the welcoming atmosphere, and then the meeting itself. I had never seen a networking meeting that was so engaged with its members. I was used to the meetings that were designed for the visitors. Attending a meeting that was structured around the members and building relationships during the meeting was really unique. Now, I am an NIA® lifer!

Keith Duke
Business Owner
NIA Spring Texas Group

When you are first introduced to Network In Action, the first thing you'll hear are the seven ways that we are unique in the world of networking. However, I would argue that all seven of them boil down to just one: everything we do is built around adding value for our members, as opposed to just putting on a show for the guests. Let me demonstrate:

> 1. Our guarantee: We guarantee you a return on your investment so that you know upfront that you aren't taking a gamble with your investment. In addition, your professional leader enters into a partnership with you to ensure that you receive that ROI.
>
> 2. Professional leadership instead of a volunteer: You are entering into a real partnership. Your franchise owner or community builder is someone who is committed to ensuring your success. In addition, the group maintains its numbers and

value indefinitely, so you don't have to worry about what we refer to as the annual networking roller-coaster.

3. Ongoing coaching: Monthly coaching sessions are designed to help you continue to grow and improve your business in a variety of ways. You never have to choose between coaching and networking again.

4. Monthly meetings held in the afternoon instead of weekly morning meetings: This makes it easier for you to work it into your schedule. In addition, this means that more business owners are making the time to come instead of sending their salespeople, which improves the quality of our membership across the board.

5. Technology: We use technology so that it's easier for you to pass and receive referrals and stay connected without face-to-face meetings.

6. Marketplace: The NIA® marketplace gives you a place to offer your unique promotions to all of our hundreds of members across the entire country. This is free marketing to an audience that has already been qualified.

7. Refer with confidence: Each member completes a background check and a personality profile so that you can refer to your personal network of friends, family members, and colleagues with confidence. In addition, it allows us to screen members before they join to ensure that you are guaranteed to be part of a group of high-caliber individuals.

Everything we do is about you! That is no accident. As I sat down and spent hours combing through the on-line reviews of networking groups, I made a list of all the things that people hated about the popular networking groups out there, and then I set out to create the exact opposite. It's really no surprise that we've been able to create an organization that people love.

> **"Joining NIA® has been one of the best things I have ever done for growing my business"**
>
> *I find Network In Action meetings to be the fastest ninety minutes of every month. I look forward to going to the meetings to meet other business people who want to grow their businesses as much as I want to grow mine. The content of the meetings is always excellent, and I always leave meetings with something beneficial that will help me grow my business. I often leave meetings thinking that we have networked more in one monthly meeting than we do in four or five of my other weekly meetings where so much time is wasted impressing the guest.*
>
> *I have belonged to many networking groups, and I find the quality of the membership of NIA® to be far superior to all other groups I have belonged to. The website and app are extremely useful tools that keep me in touch with other members. I like that the owners have a vested interest in my success. I can attest to the greatness of NIA®, as I put on eleven new clients in about a year's time—all of whom were referrals from members of NIA®. To say that the return on investment has been great is an understatement of epic proportion. I can truly say that joining NIA® has been one of the best things I have ever done for growing my business.*
>
>
> **Robert Younger**
> **On Hold Marketing, Owner**
> **NIA® Galleria Group**
>

Be Our Guest, Be Our Guest

Other networking meetings are a dog and pony show for guests. The meeting's focus is aimed at increasing the group's membership, and that is done by convincing visitors that they have to join. The entire structure of the weekly meeting is geared toward that purpose. As a member, that should be insulting.

Think about it. All the members stand and give their elevator pitches, one at a time. Do I need to hear this every single week of the year? Do I really need to hear the pest control guy say, "Hi, I'm Joe with Joe's Pest Control, and I kill bugs dead" over and over again?

There are literally thousands of hours being wasted every week all across the globe as members of networking groups are required to sit

Member-Centered Everything

back and watch as members stand up and (re)spout their company line with the only goal being to impress the guests so that the group will grow by some percent of the number of whatever warm bodies have shown up that day. Sometimes I wonder what people sitting in those networking groups are really thinking while so much of their precious time is being wasted. Next time you are in one of those meetings, watch how many members are either holding side-bar conversations or mimicking what the member is saying for the fifty-second week in a row.

Then they move on to the main attraction: announcing how many leads have been passed around. This benign ritual creates an unhealthy networking environment. As a God-loving Catholic, I sure don't want to have to stand up in front of the church and confess my sins every week. Why would I want to do that with my networking group? This results in horrible leads being passed, just for the sake of avoiding the public humiliation of admitting you don't have one to share! You wouldn't dare have zero to pass on, so you either dig up some name and number of some guy you don't even know or, if you don't have a referral to pass, you are required to say something great about the organization. That way the members are impressed because they see either a lead being passed—which might as well be monopoly money—or they hear a testimonial from a Kool-Aid drinker.

> **"NIA® is the best networking group that I know of"**
>
> NIA® is the best networking group that I know of. The contacts are great, but the business that I've gained is even better!
>
> **Darren Barr**
> **BCT Houston**

As a member, you know this going in to each meeting. You are no longer excited when someone puts that slip of pink paper into your hand. It is more likely to be fool's gold than a referral with value. However, you sit through this, week after week, because this is the only way you know how to network. Until now, this has been the best option you have had.

You agree to the song and dance as a member because you need those warm bodies to join just as desperately as the next person. That's because these groups are rife with people with the popcorn mentality—that if you don't leave with a sale today, you've wasted your time. That environment is not conducive to building long-term relationships of trust that will bring you a return. That means that after you've gathered the low-hanging fruit from the current members, you need more members.

So, you play along and continue to go through the motions, week after mind-numbing week. After all, the guests don't know that you are passing garbage or that maybe you really don't believe the company line. A percentage of those guests, regardless of how few, *will* decide to jump in, and the cycle repeats itself. And if they are members long enough, they can even become your next group leader!

And with that, another sucker is born, and the ritual continues.

At NIA®, we haven't just improved on that model. We have chosen to go in an entirely different direction because a more mature approach to building out a group is expected from today's business owners.

A Different Type of Meeting

We have crafted a model that is 100 percent focused on our members' success and growth, both personally and professionally. We believe that when we lead with this kind of value and integrity, the membership will naturally grow.

Our members know that when they step into an NIA® meeting, 100 percent of the attention will be on them and that everything that happens within those ninety minutes is

> **"What great NIA® meetings!"**
>
> *What a great NIA® meet today! We actually played Family Feud centered around the members' personal information, and it was a blast. Learning so much about each other, networking with prime business owners, and having Scott Talley there—well, it just doesn't get much better. I love the creativity in every Network In Action meeting.*
>
> **Angela Dillon**
> **Embellishments By Angela**
> **NIA® The Woodlands Group**

geared toward helping them grow their businesses. There is no wasted time impressing guests with make believe. Our franchise owners are the membership committee, and trust me when I say they are trained and prepared to run professional groups the way today's business owners expect them to be run.

4
Guaranteed ROI

In 1962, David Oreck was selling heavy upright vacuum cleaners to hotels all across the United States. During his many business travels, he noticed hotel housekeepers struggling to drag big, heavy vacuum machines all over the hotel property. The drudgery of it was clear as they pulled and pushed their way from one floor to the next. One day, he had a radical idea: What if someone were to design a lightweight, yet powerful, vacuum cleaner to relieve the physical stress of hotel staff all over the world? He approached his employers and tried to convince them to do just that.

As he tells it, he was laughed out of the room and told, "No one would ever buy a lightweight vacuum cleaner."

The Oreck Corporation began as a manufacturer of upright vacuum cleaners for the US hotel industry in 1963. It was a huge success. Bigger than he'd anticipated. Not only did hotels eagerly start buying them, but the hotel staff members themselves started buying these vastly-improved vacuum cleaners for their own use at home. So, David's original idea evolved as the Oreck Corporation began selling its unique products to residential consumers as well. As they say, now you know the rest of the story.

Well, not quite.

In 2005, I was dating a woman who sold her candle company to none other than Mr. David Oreck himself. One weekend shortly after the purchase of the candle company, she and I were invited to spend a day on David's private ranch. The property is breathtaking, with longhorns grazing along the side of his personal runway and an airplane hangar that houses over fifteen restored vintage aircrafts. During the early part of the day, we took turns flying with him in various aircraft around Louisiana and Mississippi. Once the keys to the various planes were locked away, Mr. Oreck proceeded to break out the scotch. That afternoon, he introduced me to fine whiskey and began to ask about my business. I explained to him that we were operating in thirty-seven states and two providences in Canada and that we were in the business of putting our hands into your pockets and legally extracting as much cash as possible.

I remember his response like it was yesterday. "Oh, you are in marketing? What type of business do you think I own?"

I immediately responded, "The vacuum cleaner business, of course!"

"No, not even close." he replied.

I followed up with the marketing answerer I thought he was looking for. "You are in the business of extracting dusts from people's floors." I really thought I had him there.

But again, he quickly retorted, "Nope."

I thought a moment. "Well, you now own a candle business."

"Nope."

I was clueless, but the scotch was still being poured, and it didn't look like he was going to run out any time soon, so I was happy to let him win. He went on to share stories of risk and reward and the story of his personal journey to success. He told me how, when he was in his fifties, he ventured away from the big corporate job to offer the vacuum cleaners that his boss said no one would buy. As he spoke, I was thinking about how it must have taken real courage to leave a cushy corporate gig like that—and I was glad he did. Otherwise, I'm not sure I would have just enjoyed the literal ride of my life on his planes, and the scotch may not have been quite as smooth.

However, I still did not know the correct answer to his question. I suspected it was hidden somewhere in his stories, but it continued to evade me. As we got ready to leave that day, I had to ask.

"Mr. Oreck, you never told me what business you are in. What is it?"

He smiled and clapped me on the shoulder. "Scott, I am in the 100 percent money-back guarantee business! Every Oreck vacuum cleaner comes with a 30-day, no-risk guarantee." He beamed with pride. "If you can ever figure out how to offer a money-back guarantee on your marketing, you, too, will own your own airplanes."

A World of Risk

Entrepreneurs are known for taking risks, their out-of-the-box innovations, and their "if I build it, they will come" mentality. These are real aspects of being in the business of growing businesses, but all of these attributes also come with a ton of risks. What if your risks don't pan out? What if your innovation is a flop? What if you build it and they *don't* come? The "what if" questions seem to follow business owners everywhere they turn. This is equally true for your business marketing investments. As soon as you write that check or plop down that credit card, you have assumed all the risk.

> **"I received five times my investment in the first six months"**
>
> *Three years later, I am still being rewarded for my decision to join NIA®. Not only financially, where I received five times my investment in the first six months, but also in the relationships that I have formed. As a guy who is self-employed, it is important to make every dollar count. This has been a big boom for my LegalShield business.*
>
> **Neil McGlone**
> **LegalShield, Agent**
> **NIA® Heights Group**

In the old days, when it came to marketing, the guy who could afford the largest Yellow Page ad won. It's no wonder why the yellow book companies spent millions of dollars on sales training every year. I would argue that if closing hard is what made one a good sales person, the Yellow Page reps where the best ever. Unfortunately, however, being a good sales person didn't mean you were a *good* salesperson. Promises were made that were never kept. Money poured from your bank account as you paid the price of delayed books, the wrong placement of permanent ads, or horrible art and graphics. What was done was done. There was no way to reverse it, and you were in a contract that required you to continue to pay—sometimes thousands of dollars per month.

The next year, after you were promised a credit, the reps would come back to you and convince you that all of those problems could be solved and avoided by a bigger budget—"If you just invest more with me this year, you'll be taken care of." The phone would ring off the wall, and business owners would bite like a big mouth bass.

For the next six to ten months, you were paying those increased prices while people were still using their old yellow books with tattered corners and hand-written notes throughout. What was the point?

The third year, the reps would show up and convince you that the book took time to work and your competitors were not backing off. In fact, they were now in more sections with bigger ads and, oh yeah, didn't you want the three regional Yellow Page books now being offered in the outlying areas, or did you want your competitor down the street to get all that business?

At the end of the day, you were taking all the risks—and they were not very calculated risks at that. It was really more like legal grand larceny. Even though the yellow books are a thing of the past, these practices still run rampant throughout the marketplace.

Today, there are so many different avenues where you can spend (and lose) your marketing and advertising budget. It is said that the average business owner receives six to eight phone calls every week from marketing reps. You can spend hundreds to thousands of dollars per month on SEO campaigns, Facebook advertising, traveling to networking events, paying for listings in business directories, Google AdWords, lead generation, contextual marketing, and on and on. There are hordes of people and services, all lined up to vie for your cherished marketing budget. Many of these are new ideas that you may not be familiar with, and you're nervous to spend money on an unproven system.

> **"My membership was paid for in the first meeting!"**
>
> *Thank you for inviting me to join your NIA® Columbia group. My membership was paid for in the first meeting! I specialize in performance coaching based on the MindScan. At the first meeting, I was able to schedule MindScans with everyone in the room. Within the first three people, I signed enough work to pay for my NIA® membership, and I still have the remaining MindScans to finish! Needless to say, NIA® has my full endorsement.*
>
> **Jarrod Haning**
> **Mindset Performance Coach**
> **NIA® Capitol Columbia Group**

On the other hand, some of them may be getting your ad dollars because you *are* familiar with them, but they don't give you the return on your investment you're looking for. However, you continue to invest because the familiarity feels safe to you. You are buying predictability. I recently asked a family restaurant owner in the suburbs why he advertises weekly in a music publication geared towards cult music. He said, "I started in that publication twelve years ago. I don't think we get any business from there, but I am scared to change."

The truth is that it would be nice if you could take some of the risk out of where you put your time, resources, and energy so that you can save your risk-taking for another day. It would be a welcome change to be able to cut out the trial and error with your marketing dollars. It's tiring to have to always first plant your money to see what it grows—if it grows at all. Wouldn't it be nice if there was a guarantee *before* you spent your first ad dollar? Wouldn't you like to be certain that your investment would come back to you, and then some?

The NIA Guarantee

After thinking about Mr. Oreck's challenge for over fifteen years, I was finally able to come up with a way to offer a guarantee in marketing, which is now a reality for every NIA® member. At NIA®, the franchise owners sign off on the risk *you* used to take. Before you sign your NIA® application, you and your group leader discuss and come to an agreement on what your positive ROI must be, based on shared expectations. It is *always* based on what the two of you both agree on.

The amount can vary by industry, but in most cases, we try and get to a ten-time return on your investment. Imagine heading to a casino and plopping down fifteen hundred dollars on a poker game and being guaranteed a payday of fifteen thousand dollars! Not too many people would turn that opportunity down.

Once you come to an agreement on what your ROI should be, you then receive a written guarantee that you will get that back over the course of your one-year membership. We make certain that each party has reasonable expectations and then, together, we set out to deliver on those expectations. As part of a partnership, your job is to show up and refer. Our job is to build a dynamic group that makes it easy for you to do so.

> **"I made a positive return on my investment before my check was even cashed"**
>
> *I knew within five minutes of meeting Daniel Andrews, the leader of the local group here in Columbia, SC, that this was the group for me. As soon as I heard about the guarantee, I knew that he would personally be vested into my success and that, unlike everything else I was considering putting my money into, this would not be a gamble for me. I was right! I made a positive return on my investment before my check was even cashed, as Daniel gave me my first referral within twenty-four hours of our first meeting.*
>
> **Gwen Weiler**
> **Book Editor/Ghostwriter**
> **NIA® Capitol Columbia Group**

I spent almost three decades working with business owners, helping them make the best investments possible with their marketing budgets. I still am. At NIA®, we enjoy giving you a guaranteed ROI on your investment. If we miss, your second year is free.

This is not an empty promise. It has been tried and tested with hundreds of members—many of whom are in your exact industry. Out of the hundreds of members who have enrolled, we have had to offer the second year free to only four members to date.

We can confidently offer this guarantee because we know our model works and our leaders are qualified to show you exactly how to get the

ROI you're looking for. When it comes to your membership, we don't just set it and forget it. Your leader takes an active role in ensuring your success. Whether your leader is scouting out the talent and the clients you're looking for or sitting down with you for a private one-to-one, your leader has been trained on exactly how to help you move the needle.

From Moose Rosenfeld: A Franchise Owner

One of the things that attracted me to Network In Action as a franchise model was their ROI guarantee on the annual investment. Coming from the radio and Internet marketing industries, I was never able to offer that. It really seemed impossible to make an offer like that, but the reality is that it works quite well. I operate two groups and have only had one member who, after twelve months, did not hit our agreed upon goal.

It works because the members' attendance stays up because of their desire to keep the guarantee in place, which has a positive effect on everything we are trying to achieve, both as a group and as individuals. We are each committed to our success as individuals and to the success of the collective group. In addition, I can use our software to track the activity of each member. That means I can head off a problem before it happens. If Bob isn't bringing in or getting referrals, I know well before the end of the year that I need to sit down with him and do some coaching or some cheerleading—whatever it takes to help him reach his goals.

This is the thing I like the most as a franchisee. The guaranteed ROI helps create a relationship between my member and me. We both enter into a marketing relationship as partners focused on achieving our goals collectively. It is a win-win for both of us!

It Works for Every Industry – Not Every Individual

Networking works for every industry, but not every individual. This means that networking has the power to transform your business endeavors, but only as far as you, the individual, will allow it to. We had a guy, a business coach, who had been in our organization for two years and didn't feel like he was getting any value from his membership. I asked him why he didn't feel like he'd gotten more out of his relationship with NIA® because I could look around at other people in

Guaranteed ROI

> **"I have added twelve new clients"**
>
> *I would like to give a shout out to my group leader, Moose Rosenfeld, for putting together a networking group that really works. In less than two years, I have added twelve wonderful new clients. To all of our clients, thank you so much for your trust and for allowing me and my team to serve you. Thanks, Moose. NIA® really works!*
>
> **Robert Younger**
> **On Hold Marketing, Owner**
> **NIA® Galleria Group**

his exact industry in other NIA® groups who were getting tremendous benefits. It's clearly not a question of his industry. It is often the individual who is the problem. He casually admitted, "You know, I didn't do a good job reaching out to other people and building relationships." He admitted that he hadn't done a good job getting to know the other members, hadn't taken the time to reach out and help people, and hadn't been passing referrals. These facts scream why he wasn't receiving the benefits. The reality is that if you do a good job passing referrals and taking care of others, they are going to go out of their ways to figure out how they can reciprocate.

At NIA®, we work to help you transform the way you're currently networking so that it feels comfortable and will naturally lead to you achieving your stated goals. The bottom line is that if you are keeping your end of the bargain by coming to meetings and passing referrals, you are going to earn a positive return on your investment. Guaranteed! If you find that your networking efforts are not paying dividends, then there are likely two things you need to do:

1. Make sure you're giving. Are you showing up with the intention to give? Or are you expecting to sit back and collect referrals overnight without the investment required to build a relationship? At NIA®, we strategically aim to create a culture of giving and reciprocity. We will discuss those ideals in later chapters, but the point is that you need to show up. Don't just come in body. Walk through those doors with your head and heart in the game of giving, and it *will* be returned to you.

Gary Cooper, a CPA in my area, came to his first meeting, missed his second, and then after his third meeting, told me, "NIA® is not going to work." Now, this was a guy who had moved to Houston and would readily offer the details on how he built his CPA practice by starting his own networking group! In fact, he still offers a free networking event once a month called Band Jam where music-loving business owners gather at his office to drink, eat, sing, and network for free.

> **"I have definitely received far more on my ROI guarantee than my annual investment"**
>
> *What I love most about NIA® is the quality of people in the network. I have definitely received far more on my ROI guarantee than my annual investment.*
>
> **Ruth Mallon**
> **Storyteller Promotions, Owner**
> **NIA® Galleria Group**

I explained to Gary in great detail that it was impossible to build trust in just one meeting, and it is even more difficult when you skip meetings, which shows that you're placing your own priorities over those of the group. After some reluctance, he agreed to stay in the group. Within a year, he had received over twenty referrals and several thousand dollars in new accounts. Soon after, he put two additional CPAs in other NIA® groups around the city and bought an NIA® franchise for his son to operate. Now, that is what I call a success story!

2. Wait for the outcome to catch up with your effort. If you are showing up to the meetings and you are giving—if you're doing everything your leader has coached you to do—then it is just a matter of time before your efforts pay off. You have to trust the process and know that the outcome has already been determined by your actions.

My wife, Moriah, had a slow start to her success with NIA®, but what she didn't realize was that while she was waiting, the effects of her passing referrals to others were about to have a dramatic impact on her real estate business. She says:

> When I first started attending NIA® meetings as the residential realtor in the group, I was discouraged because I

wasn't getting any referrals. I started to wonder if I was being intentionally left out because I'm married to Scott. I talked to him about my concerns, and he told me to just keep going and taking care of people, and eventually I would be taken care of, too.

I took his advice and kept going, and I made a positive effort to give. Within about two weeks, the office supply guy in our group, Darren Barr, called and said, "I'd like to bring my next-door neighbor to your house. He's from El Salvador. He speaks English, but his native language is Spanish, and I know you are fluent." At the time, I thought he was just setting up a friendly chat.

So, I met with his neighbor, and the short version of the story is that he had a connection with a lady in Costa Rica who had a $400 million concrete quarry for sale that he needed help marketing in America. I ended up with a partial listing on this property that will bring in over $2.5 million in commissions when the property sells! Additionally, two other members of that same group have listed properties with me that will bring in about $17,000 in commissions.

Even though my wife, who was the inspiration behind NIA®, didn't get any referrals during her first seven months, she continued to go and give from her heart without worrying about what she was getting back. She did everything she was coached to do and stayed positive. As a result, she is now sitting on a life-changing opportunity because of a relationship she built with one member of the group—a member who had nothing to do with real estate or the concrete quarry. To this day, he has never personally given my wife a direct business referral for a real estate transaction. But he is the one who connected my wife with one of the largest real estate transactions going on in Costa Rica right now.

This is the true magic of networking. I often hear people say that they are not sure about the members in a particular group, which tells me they are completely missing the point. The real value lies in who those members know through church, school, Facebook, or LinkedIn connections. Even though you can't be certain about the timing of your ROI or exactly how it will look when it happens, when you follow the NIA® model, you can be certain that it will happen—or your next year is on us!

5
Professional Community Builders vs. Volunteers

Most major networking group in America is run by a volunteer or is a non-profit organization. The fact that we have paid leadership is a unique identifier of Network In Action. However, for our franchise owners, the money always follows their passion for building a successful group. It truly is *not* about the money. It is about creating value for our members—it is about creating value for you.

Look at it this way: You can get your nephew to build you a website, or you can pay someone to build it. The professional, trained expert you pay is always going to do a better job. Period. This principle is true for everything. When you ask someone to give you something for free, you are likely to get what you paid for. In a typical networking group today, the group is run by the next man or woman up, which is most often determined by who served as last year's volunteer vice president. This annual migration of leadership leaves many groups wandering aimlessly while the new leaders find their way. A volunteer lawyer, CPA, realtor, or whoever it is who is next up is just not going to care as much about a networking group as a vested professional. With NIA®, we are breaking the mold and doing things a different way. We are proving that better leaders build better groups!

We aren't just simply paying our leaders. We aren't offering a job opportunity with rebates on enrollments. Our groups are set up as franchisees with owners who have to first make an investment in order to have the rights to operate an NIA® group. These investments are not made lightly, and they ensure your leaders' commitment to the purpose and integrity of NIA's model.

Each franchise owner is a professionally-trained Community Builder, which means they are every bit "the professional" you would look for when hiring for any other task in your business.

Focused on YOU

Our franchise owners have a financial stake in the success of the group. That means that in addition to taking the time to help your business grow, they are personally invested into making sure it does. They are always thinking ahead on your behalf. They understand that your success is necessary for the group's success. They want to make sure you have every opportunity possible to build relationships with the types of business owners and decision makers who can impact your business in a positive way. When NIA® franchise owners leave a monthly meeting, they are typically leaving and going right back to work on group-building strategies.

> **"My group leader is the reason our group is successful"**
>
> *Network In Action has a great way to connect and network with other local businesses. My group leader, Barbara Anne, is by far the most aggressive—in a good way—and organized of the several leaders that I have been under. Her groups are successful, and I believe that she is the reason.*
>
> **Sean Priddy**
> **Alexaur, Representative**
> **NIA® Katy Connectors Group**

By joining the NIA® group, you essentially hire a professional matchmaker to keep an eye out for the people looking for your products or services. This completely takes the risk out of your investment and is a service that is unique to NIA®.

Sure, in other groups your fellow group members have your name in their Rolodexes, and hopefully you are on their radar so that when they come across someone who is looking for what you have to offer, they will be quick to pass along your name. That has great value and is why networking has a long history of working, even when run by volunteers. However, the volunteer group leaders are just like you: they have full-time obligations with either their employment or running their own businesses. Although they are giving and may be sincerely committed to the group, their first priority is the same as yours—making sure they pay their own bills. At the end of the day, they have no real incentive to create a dynamic and growing group.

NIA® group leaders, on the other hand, are not just saving your name for those moments they come across referrals for you. They are actively *looking* for people to connect you with. You magnify your networking power a hundred-fold by enlisting their help. I promise they are going to more networking events than you are. Every time they step into a new room of entrepreneurs, they are representing you. They are your eyes and ears when your eyes and ears are busy doing other things. Together, you are able to divide and conquer. It is their job to think about you and the exact resources, people, and tools that will help *you* take your business to the next level.

> **"It is great to be in a networking group with a professional leader"**
>
> *My group leader, Moose Rosenfeld, has a wealth of knowledge, and I highly recommend setting up a one-on-one with him today! It is great to be in a networking group with a professional leader.*
>
> **Robert Younger**
> **On Hold Marketing, Owner**
> **NIA® Galleria Group**

This is what shapes the itinerary for each monthly meeting, the supplemental group networking events, and their recruiting efforts. In addition to staying focused on creating a dynamic group that is most often larger than volunteer-run groups, they are strategically creating a network of individuals who are compatible in their ability to help each other. For instance, if you're a residential realtor who has just joined, you better believe your leader is going to be on the hunt for a reputable mortgage lender and a real estate attorney. If you are an online marketer, your leader is going to be on the lookout for copywriters, graphic designers, and web developers who can help to support your needs and feed referrals into your growing enterprise.

What sets you apart in your industry? Who is your ideal client? What is your ideal secondary contact—someone who is likely to be able to refer your ideal client to you? What problems are you trying to solve in your business? These are the points of the most interest to your group leader—more so than your ability to sign a check. This is not a numbers game. This is a game of strategy, and they only win when you do.

The Networking Rollercoaster

Would you let a volunteer manage your SEO, print materials, website, marketing campaign, or relationships? We have proven that not only is a professionally-run group larger and more active, it is also simply more efficient and better! Having paid leadership creates more consistency and value across the board. It eliminates what we call the "networking rollercoaster" that is characteristic of every single group being run by a volunteer.

With volunteers heading up operations, you never know if you're going to be up or down, barreling ahead at high speed, or on the sure-and-steady descent when leadership changes every October. This happens annually all over the country. There is simply no way every volunteer has the same skill, passion, or time to run the group as the last leader. You are always on the rollercoaster—always on the way up or on the way down—but your dues stay the same even when your results suffer.

Let's say you joined an early-morning group two years ago because you were impressed with their bulging membership or their charismatic leader. How's that group doing today? Regardless, there is no guarantee on how it will be doing next month, next year, or two years from now. The reason is because "volunteer leadership" is equivalent to "transient

> **"He doesn't bring on warm bodies to fill a quota—he cares about the quality of the membership"**
>
> *What I love about my NIA® group is my leader's enthusiasm and ability to bring together good, high-quality small business owners so that we can help each other grow our businesses. All of our members are either owners or decision makers, and that makes a difference when networking. Moose does not bring on warm bodies to fill a quota. He cares about the quality of the membership.*
>
> **Cass McNinch**
> **Aberdeen Building Group**
> **NIA® Galleria Group**

leadership." When leadership changes, everything changes. I know of a weekly group here locally that was booming with forty-one members at one time. However, as soon as the volunteer leader stepped down and another volunteer took his place, the numbers plummeted.

The success of any group is dependent on the perceived value of the group (mostly from guests who are invited to attend). That perception is largely dependent on the skill sets and participation of the leader. When you walk into the room and a new volunteer is now heading up the group, the entire dynamic shifts. This creates an environment ripe for drama and politics to sneak in and start eating away at the integrity of the group.

In NIA®, the leadership never changes because each group is being led by a franchise owner—someone who has made a financial investment into doing this for a living. You don't have to worry about their excitement sagging because the comped membership dues don't seem worth it anymore. No—they are committed to showing up today, tomorrow, and forever with the single goal of helping you grow your business.

Leaders Alone Are Responsible for Growth

When you join a volunteer-run networking group, you become one of the volunteers, too. Think about it: You go to a meeting early one morning, and you are impressed with the energy and the number of referrals being passed around (though the powdered eggs are hard to choke down). The leader is charismatic enough to get you laughing before you've had that first cup of coffee. The members recognize that you're a guest, so everyone is on their best behavior in order to convince you this is the group for you. This is great! You sign up.

Uh oh. You've crossed over from being a "guest" to being a "member." Now the pressure is on for you to help grow the group, too. Who do you know, who do you know, who do you know? If the group shrinks, everyone suffers, so you have to pull your weight and make sure everyone's investment—including yours—is paying off. Whatever you do, don't let the membership go down!

When you are part of a volunteer organization, each member holds some responsibility for growing and maintaining the group membership numbers. The group itself becomes a member that you're trying to pass referrals to. This dilutes what should be your main focus, which is to bring referrals to the group members alone. In addition, it's harder than you think. You quickly realize that it's more than just a numbers game. As a member, you are now "behind the curtain." You now see that this bulging group of participants is buzzing with sales people selling, multi-level marketers recruiting, and employees needing to meet quotas—all are welcome! But there's one big problem: those are not, and will never be, your best networking partners.

When you have a paid leader, these are non-issues. Our franchise owners are required to keep their rosters at over twenty-five members, and the leader alone focuses on growing and managing the group so that you can keep the singular focus of serving your friends.

Corporately Trained Networking Experts

You can be sure that each group leader is a networking expert qualified to train you how to enhance your networking skills and to help you get the most out of your group membership. In most instances, we look for the most connected business owners in an area to develop our franchises. These leaders are typically your number-one referral source. Working with them is the equivalent of adding an additional sales person to your payroll—but incredibly less expensive.

Each franchise owner is required to participate in a rigorous training program to ensure they meet our five-star standard of excellence. In addition to having a thorough grasp of the art of networking, these are professionals who have mastered the business world in their own right. They are able to draw on their wide

> **"Everyone else is just a bonus"**
>
> *Joining this group has magnified my networking power a hundred-fold. My partnership with my group leader, Daniel Andrews, alone would make it worth my time because he is always scouting for me. Everyone else is just a bonus.*
>
> **Gwen Weiler**
> **Book Editor/Ghostwriter**
> **NIA® Capitol Columbia Group**

spectrum of knowledge, resources, and contacts to help you strategize your own growth.

In the next chapter, I'm going to introduce you to three of these leaders and let them personally tell you a little more about themselves.

6
Meet Our Leaders

The single most important task I have is vetting people who want to run a Network In Action group. When we get that right, everything else falls into place. One of the many things I love about what we are doing at NIA® is that we have a singleness of purpose when we look for our franchise owners. It really is simple. I look for people who love helping others! People who have led before and know what it means to lead. People who wake up every day asking, "What I can do today to help the businesses that have entrusted their hard-earned marketing dollars and, even more important, their time to me?" They recognize that for some business members, this may be the only funds they will put towards marketing in any given year. We all take that extremely seriously.

Our leaders have to both agree to and relish having the opportunity to help their members and the communities where our groups hold meetings. All of our franchise owners act as their very own membership committees. More important, they are guaranteeing every member's investment. To date, we have been really blessed to partner with and award our franchises to very high-quality individuals.

I recently received a call from one of our most successful and passionate franchise owners, Stacy Harris. She is the leader of four groups in Houston, where she serves in The Woodlands area. She was calling to inform me that 100 percent of her members in two of her groups were renewing for their second year. While it would be unfair to expect this result with every group, it was not all that surprising. Why wouldn't a business owner want to continue to develop a relationship with one of the most networked individuals in town?

Stacy embellishes every quality we look for in an owner. She is goal-oriented and people-driven with a long history of experience with networking. Her resume includes having been heavily involved as a volunteer with BNI®, serving in a number of capacities, including Vice President, President, and Ambassador—all of which were volunteer efforts that resulted in her dues being waived! (She was rewarded for her service by being threatened with a lawsuit over an illegal non-compete that BNI® forced her to sign.) So, it is not surprising that she has added over 110 businesses to three groups in the last twelve months.

Like I said, my job is easy. I just have to find people who love helping others and are committed to providing them with the NIA® formula for successfully connecting people. Now I want to introduce you to three of our leaders, including Stacy, and let them tell you a little more about themselves.

Moose Rosenfeld, *First franchisee*
NIA Galleria Group, Houston, Texas
NIA Bellaire Group, Bellaire, Texas

My father, Dickie, served as president and general manager of KILT, one of the most iconic radio stations in Houston, Texas. He spent thirty-eight years in the industry. This had a profound impact on me. I eventually got into radio sales in 1974 in San Antonio, Texas, and took the same path as my father, working my way up to sales manager and general manager roles at radio stations across the country. I learned that when you're new to a market, you have to get to know people. I was blessed with a personality to have never met a stranger. I have always found it very easy to meet people, and that's still true to this day.

I have worked with businesses on the local level my entire career. From radio to Internet marketing, I have always had a passion for helping a business get more customers. I have always been the idea guy.

Building Relationships That Last a Lifetime

Great ideas can sell lots of product. I'm still an idea guy today, but working with a different kind of product—people.

After my dad passed in 2000, radio was not the same to me. I retired from radio in 2003 and became on entrepreneur. I joined my first business networking group, Cooper Connection, in 2005. The idea of having a fellow member either use me or refer me was pretty remarkable. I got a lot of value out of the group. I still have friendships I developed at Cooper Connection and do business with several of them to this day. The group was run by an outstanding networker, Joann Cooper. At one time, she ran eight different chapters. I learned a great deal from her on how to run a great meeting. I was a member for a little over five years until Joann decided to shut it down in 2010.

I was a member of BNI® Memorial for over five years and made some great friends during that time, too. I served on the membership committee twice and filled the secretary/treasurer role before accepting an Ambassador role. I passed lots of referrals to our membership over the years.

When Scott Talley called me in November 2014 to tell me his idea of a new networking group he was starting called Network In Action, I personally thought he had gone crazy. Going up against the big guys? Was he kidding? However, I trusted him enough to investigate. After all, I know if you can't dream it, it will never happen.

I came to his NIA® Heights launch in January 2015 and was impressed with his membership. I went to his February and March meetings, still as an observer. He was at well over thirty members and growing!

After much soul searching, I decided in late March to move forward with being the first NIA® franchisee. It was a step of faith and a step for my future. I announced my decision to drop my membership with my BNI® group at the April meeting, much to the surprise of the members. I was always there. I had been part of their sales team for years. And now, no more Moose.

I launched NIA® Galleria in July 2015 and NIA® Bellaire the following January. Today, I have over sixty members representing many different industries. This has been very rewarding to me. I love working for my members. As the head of the membership committee, I get to decide who becomes part of my groups. Because of our business model, the vast majority of my members are either business owners or decision makers, which I think in itself is very cool.

My Leadership Principles

In a sense, building out an NIA® Group is like building a great radio station. You win in Radio by having great talent—you win in networking groups by having great members. I know without a shadow of a doubt that my members are my "Why." There's a saying, "Knowledge is power." I think knowing a thousand people with knowledge is a lot *more* powerful! This is what I truly believe I was put on this planet to do:

- Run an outstanding business referral group
- Build by having dynamic members
- Build by having a great business model
- Build by having awesome technology
- Build by doing this full time
- Build by caring more about my members than myself

I am so blessed to be able to do this. I thank Scott for his vision, his passion to serve, his family values, and simply sharing NIA® with me. This has been the most rewarding time of my life. My tombstone will read: Moose Rosenfeld - Super Networker.

Keith Duke, *NIA Pioneer*
NIA Spring Texas Group

My journey to becoming a professional networker with Network In Action has been an action-filled adventure. To tell the full story, I must go back quite a few years. I barely made it out of high school. I was the guy who would rebel against the system just to test it. I would wear sunglasses, show up to class two seconds after the bell, and ask question after question about assignments. Let's just say that the principles all knew my name, and I went to a high school of nearly four thousand students, so you really had to work hard for *all* of the principles to know your name.

I tell that part of my story because testing the system is why I believe my path has taken me to entrepreneurship. I have worked for "the man" in the corporate world and, though I learned a lot, it was not my thing.

I have had several business ventures—from direct sales, to construction, to consulting—and now Network In Action. I came across Network In Action while running my construction and concrete business. It was such a great opportunity I couldn't pass it up. I had been in an organized networking organization for several years, and it had run its course for me. I started to look for what else was out there, and as a good networker, I reached out to my network circle to see what they could refer. A mutual business professional introduced me to NIA®. I set up a time to go to a meeting and see what it was all about.

When I arrived at the meeting, I was instantly blown away. The energy, the people, the welcoming atmosphere, and then the meeting itself. I had never seen a networking meeting that was so engaged with its members. I was used to meetings that were designed for the visitors. Attending a meeting that was structured around the members and building relationships during the meeting was really unique. However, even though I was there as a visitor, I still came away with loads of information. That meeting was run by Scott Talley. He gave me the complete rundown of what NIA® was all about. The things that really caught my attention were the monthly meetings, full-time leadership, and state-of-the-art technology. I had been a member of an organization that was stuck in the Stone Age and had no vision of moving into the twenty-first century. It was amazing that there could be a higher level of networking with proven results on a modern platform. When he told me about the franchise opportunity, he had me hooked. Now, I am an NIA® lifer!

My Leadership Principles

As a professional networker, I still visit other groups as a method to meet and grow my network. It is just something I believe we have to constantly do. If we as franchise owners are not improving our networking skills and growing our connections, we are not providing the best service to our members. As I attend these other events, it is so apparent how well NIA® is organized and structured to bring the best networking experience to its members.

My time in NIA® has been amazing. I have been very fortunate to be involved in two franchises. I created them six months apart, and I am so proud to say that I made a return on each of those investments in less than thirty days. I worked with a colleague to start and build two groups out to great success. It occurred to us that in order to grow the NIA® name and territory, we needed to split up. So, we did! Those two existing groups are still active, growing, and doing great things.

Growing out groups has its challenges as you get further in, but the skills I have learned from such mass recruiting are skills I will cherish for a lifetime—in addition to the countless connections and contacts that I've made, which are growing on a daily basis. I have been very fortunate to be a part of Network In Action and count my blessings daily to be a franchise owner. I know many professionals who are in franchised businesses and from what I can tell, no other company treats its owners as well as NIA® does. Knowing my entrepreneur spirt, this will not be the last venture for me, but helping business professionals grow their referral-based businesses through NIA® is something that will always be on my plate.

Stacy Harris, *First franchisee to own four groups*
NIA The Woodlands Groups, Texas

I started my image consulting business, Impressions, eleven years ago after working in the sales and marketing industries for about a decade. It was a good decision. Though being an entrepreneur is fraught with uncertainty and challenges, I found that I thrived as my own boss. Of course, one of the biggest hurdles all business owners face is getting their name and product to the masses. Since I started my business on a very limited budget, my only marketing strategy was my own blood, sweat, and tears. I have always been a relationship person, and I knew that if I could just meet people face to face and develop a relationship with them, I'd be able to build my business.

Fortunately, a friend of mine invited me to a professional networking event and the rest is history. I was totally mesmerized by this group of people who were meeting together to talk about their businesses and send customers to one another through the oldest (and best) marketing method in the book—word of mouth! I loved meeting all these new people, finding out about their businesses, and then figuring out ways to connect them to customers and clients who would bring them business. Nothing made me happier than to get a call or text from my networking buddies telling me that a referral I had sent them had turned into cold, hard cash.

For the next ten years, I attended as many networking events as I could fit in, narrowed down the ones that were the most mutually beneficial, and then I committed myself to being the best networker I could be. I studied the art of networking, I talked to people who I knew were good networkers, and I read books on networking. The result? Over the years, I became a great networker with a crazy amount of contacts and connections.

There was one networking group in particular that I had dedicated myself to for nine years. I served as president of that group multiple times and was always in a leadership role of some kind over those years. I excelled at leading and inspiring the group to hit new goals and set a big vision of success. It was a great experience, and I formed valuable relationships there, but after nine years, I had outgrown the group, and it was time for me to move on.

I found out about NIA® through, guess what, a networking partner. I drove an hour to visit my first NIA® meeting in May 2016. I was so impressed with the level of professionalism I saw in the whole concept of using technology to keep everyone in touch with each other and the business that was being generated by the members.

Scott Talley was running that meeting, and I pelted him with questions after the meeting about how NIA® worked, what was the structure, and what being a franchise owner looked like. I couldn't stop thinking about that meeting, and two months later, in July 2016, I was signing the papers to become a franchise owner myself.

I started two groups simultaneously in August 2016. I have been blessed with incredible members and growth. I now have a total of 110 members between four groups!

My past experiences in leading other networking groups for years has definitely shaped me and the way I run my Network In Action groups. Because of that experience, I have a good handle on the kind of people I am looking for to be members. I also understand how important it is to have a strong, cohesive, and diverse group.

My Leadership Principles

There are a number of things I do to create value for my members. Number one, I make sure our meetings are fun! We laugh, we tease, we share our victories and successes, and I reward them for being good members.

The second thing I do is I am constantly in touch with all of my members. I make sure that every single one of my members hears from me via phone, text, or email every week. This "touch," as I call it, is not about business—it's about them as people. I'm just reaching out to make sure they are OK and that their families are good, and I always ask them what I can do for them. I check in with them and make sure they are getting out of NIA® what they want to get, and if they're not, I ask them what I can do to fix it. The result has been a 98 percent renewal rate among my members.

The third thing I do is I help to facilitate the building of relationships among my members. As I bring on new members, I suggest to them fellow members who I think will be good referral partners for them and help them connect with those people. One of the best things I've done with my groups is partner up members within their groups. I then give each partnership a homework assignment, requiring them to have a one-on-one, and to attend another networking event (not NIA®) together. I try to partner up people who I just think will like each other, have things in common, or who have similar responsibilities in their jobs. This creates a camaraderie among the members, and they become each other's' "wingmen" at the meeting they attend together. The result has been the development of some amazing relationships, and when people like each other, know each other, and trust each other, they figure out ways to do business together!

The last, and most important, thing I do for my members is pray for each and every one of my members every day. I pray for their businesses, their health, the wellbeing of their families, and their success. I truly believe that has made a huge difference in their lives.

7
Ongoing Coaching

When you're a business owner, you probably recognize the value of both coaching and networking. When you're working with a coach, you are working with someone qualified to help you navigate the proverbial road less traveled—the road between where you are and where you want to be. Even if you are in the beginning stages of creating a vision of what you want to achieve and what is possible in terms of your future, you can bet that someone has traversed that road before.

When you're networking, you are extending your reach through synergy and adding valuable contacts that are far more important than just filling a Rolodex. At the end of the day, relationships are what really matters, so networking is an essential part of growing your business.

So, both coaching *and* networking are vital to the lifeblood and efficiency of your enterprise. Often, the problem is that there are only so many dollars in your budget and only so many hours in a day. As a business owner, sales person, or entrepreneur, you are usually faced with having to choose one or the other. When you're investing time and resources into coaching, your network may not be growing. When you're working on growing and serving your network, coaching often has to wait for another day.

At NIA®, we recognize the importance of both of these, which is why we incorporate both into your membership. We have created a platform that includes ongoing business development, growth, and learning—all while helping you build relationships that last a lifetime.

Monthly Coaching Sessions

One of the added benefits of your NIA® membership is our monthly coaching sessions that we offer. These are typically free, city-wide, ninety-minute networking events in which we have one of our NIA® members, an expert in a particular field, speak on a topic where that person's experience can lend a hand to other members.

One month, it may be on sales training. Next month, it may be on keeping up with the latest trends in social media. Another month, it may be focused on helping you with your accounts receivable or cash flow. Next time, we may feature a CPA who's talking about how to put more money in your pocket and pay less in taxes.

Regardless of the topic, you get to pick and choose which events to attend. We spend about an hour on the coaching and the rest of the time networking with members and guests from across the local area—all of which is included in your annual membership.

> **"The information I have gleaned from these speakers is worth my annual membership"**
>
> *I recently volunteered to offer a seminar myself on "How Disney Uses Customer Service for Marketing." I am happy to say the seminar was attended by NIA® members from all over town. It was awesome and provided me and my company with great exposure.*
>
> *Network In Action does a great job with trainings and coaching. It only makes sense that with so many members, there is a ton of expertise in every city. NIA® brings us all together monthly for an informational coaching session. I have no doubt the information I have gleaned from these speakers is worth my annual membership.*
>
> **Mike Mallon**
> **Storyteller Promotions, Owner**
> **NIA® Bellair Group**

Each meeting is strategically organized to provide value to you as you work to increase your revenue. Although networking is at the forefront of what NIA® is about, we have many members who tell us that at the end of the day, the seminars are equally as valuable. During these meetings, we discuss topics that are timely and relevant to your current business needs. Having these discussions and asking these questions in a group setting means that you are able to draw on the experiences of each individual in attendance, and each individual is able to draw on yours.

> **"NIA® has it right!"**
>
> *I just want to thank our leader, Barbara Anne, for the opportunity to share with you about the threat of ID theft, and about my business. I would also like to acknowledge her for her leadership and the incredible job she's doing for the group. NIA® has it right with a professional leader in every group.*
>
> **Carlos Hernandez**
> **LegalShield, Representative**
> **NIA® Cyfair Connectors Group**

For example, if we are discussing marketing, part of the discussion may include questions such as: What have you found to be your most valuable forms of advertising? What have you tried, but it didn't give you a return? Was it because you were doing it wrong, or because it's an outdated strategy? What avenues have you considered, but haven't been sure they would be worth your investment? It's likely that another member who is in a similar industry as yours can share with you how to conduct a successful Facebook ad campaign. Or perhaps someone has just spent a hefty budget on Pay Per Click advertising and can speak about his return on investment. What about you? People want to know about your experiences as well.

Each monthly meeting features a new topic of discussion that is hand-selected by your group leader based on the collective interests and needs of the group.

Regardless of how successful your business is, it's important to maintain a culture of ongoing business development, learning, and growing. Things change so fast in the business world, and we want to ensure that you are always up to speed and aware of the new tools, resources, and best-business practices that will help you get to the top, and to stay there.

The Value of Networking

Building Relationships That Last a Lifetime

> **"Every member gets to show off their skills"**
>
> *One of the many things I love about NIA® is how every member gets an opportunity to show off their skills and talent. Thanks NIA®!*
>
> **Michael Reichek**
> **Financial Service**
> **NIA® W. University Group**

One of the topics we will consistently discuss in your regular monthly meeting is how to improve your networking skills. As previously mentioned, we encourage you to participate in every networking opportunity you can. Whether you're networking within NIA® or mingling at other venues, we want to ensure you are equipped to do it as effectively as possible.

There is more to networking than just getting names and numbers. So much more. In fact, as I stated before, I used to despise networking, but that was only because I didn't understand how to do it right, and I was completely turned off by how it was being offered. I didn't understand that my success was determined by my ability to build sound relationships. At NIA®, we have gleaned the most proven networking strategies in the industry, and we have drilled down on the best of the best. These are the strategies we are committed to incorporating into each monthly meeting and training you how to execute in *any* networking meeting you attend.

Qualified Networking Coaches

We do not sell franchises to just anyone with a checkbook. Our vetting process ensures that members will be put in groups where they can expect the best results and will be led by those who are qualified to coach them toward greater success. Our leaders come from various backgrounds within the business world and are able to draw on all of their valuable resources and experiences in order to help connect you with the people and

> **"One of the real benefits of NIA® is learning how to network"**
>
> *One of the real benefits of NIA® is learning how to network. This is a classy organization that does everything right.*
>
> **Fabiana Cuggionni**
> **N2 Publishing**
> **NIA® W. University Group**

50

resources you need in order to grow your business and to create a smoother ride for you as you expand.

When someone approaches us about becoming a franchise owner, there is a laundry list of things we look for. We specifically award our franchises to people who share a common goal of helping our members grow their businesses and develop their companies. However, it isn't enough for them to have the passion and drive to just do that. They have to be qualified to do so. For this reason, it is equally as important that our franchise owners are teachers and students of business. Most often, they have already run or are currently running successful organizations. This allows us to glean from their background whether they are capable of becoming the networking experts they need to be in order to carry our NIA® brand forward.

Our franchise training is extensive and ongoing. Not only do we train on every aspect of building out a group properly, we work tirelessly to make sure that our franchise owners reflect the culture that we are trying to create in our NIA® brand. So, not only must they be people of action, they must be committed to their communities as well. NIA® members enjoy the benefit of these committed, highly-trained, and vetted professionals both in regard to the on-going coaching seminars and the networking training provided.

Once you become a member, you will never have to choose between those two vital parts of growing your business again.

8
Monthly Meetings

Keith Duke sat in his chair, trying hard not to roll his eyes. It was 7:23 on a Tuesday morning. He had been up since 5:00. The drone of familiar voices around him, saying the same thing they said last week, and the week before, and the week before, made him restless in his seat. He understood the value of networking, but doing it this way—the way he'd always done it—was starting to take its toll on him.

"Before I found Network In Action, I had been in an organized networking organization for several years, and it had run its course for me. I was tired of the weekly meetings—of standing up and saying what I do every time, and if I had to hear the pest control person say he kills bugs one more time, I was going to go insane. I had to find something a step above the rest."

One of the reasons he was first drawn to sign up as an NIA® member was because of our unique model of holding meetings once a month versus once a week. In fact, this is one of the biggest reasons people are either leaving traditional networking groups and looking for an alternative.

There are thousands of people across the country who recognize the need for networking, but they either don't want to or simply can't attend weekly, early-morning networking meetings. Some people join local chapters anyway in hopes that they can make it work and then either leave or are kicked out after missing more than a couple meetings per year. Either way, the end results are the same: they just flushed hundreds of dollars in membership fees down the drain, and they are back where they started.

Monthly Meetings

There are several reasons you may not be able to consistently attend weekly gatherings: Perhaps your clients span the United States and you are required to travel often. Maybe you are the parent responsible for getting your children dressed and fed in the morning before they go to school. Many business owners are up at dawn putting out fires and don't even breathe until after lunchtime. You may be one of the majority of Americans who don't particularly like getting up before the sun. Or, perhaps you are like many others who are currently attending the weekly ritual of repetition, and you're just done with it.

> **"It was mind blowing how fast we all connected"**
>
> *When I joined Heights NIA®, I was skeptical to say the least. I am a seasoned networker and I know historically that in order to build relationships you have to invest a lot of time before you can expect referrals. Well, with NIA®'s monthly meeting agendas, it was mind blowing how fast we all connected. Now, three years later, I am still being rewarded for my decision to join.*
>
> **Neil McGlone**
> **LegalShield, Agent**
> **NIA® Heights Group**

Whatever your reasons are for not enlisting in a morning meeting, you are not alone.

This issue was one of the first pain points I identified when I was researching reviews of networking groups. The reasons for this pain are easy enough to recognize. However, what I didn't immediately see was how many benefits are associated with holding meetings once a month instead. These include:

- Saving an enormous amount of time
- Higher-quality members because owners are more likely to join instead of sending their underlings
- Expanded networking opportunities

Saving Time

The first and most obvious benefit to having a once-a-month meeting is the amount of time that you save. This networking model gives you some additional eighty-plus hours in your schedule every year. You are able to carve out more time in your life and in your business for the things that are most important without sacrificing the value of being part of an organized group of people who are all supporting each other's business growth.

Even the few hours you save every week make a big impact on your day. A recent study suggests that losing as little as thirty minutes of sleep can increase your insulin resistance, which raises your risk of diabetes and obesity. There are studies that have tracked the correlation between having to set the clocks back in the spring (i.e. losing an hour of sleep) and higher incidents of car accidents. In his article *Sleep Habits: More Important Than You Think*, clinical psychologist Michael Breus, a fellow of the American Academy of Sleep Medicine, says that reducing your nighttime sleep by as little as ninety minutes for just one night can reduce your daytime alertness by as much as 32 percent. This cuts your work productivity by almost a third! Multiply that effect by four weeks, and you're potentially losing over a days' worth of productivity every month. How much is it costing you to wake up a couple hours earlier once a week, in addition to the loss of your beauty sleep? (And let's face it—some of us need that more than others.)

> **"It's less time consuming, and I still get the same results, if not more"**
>
> *One of the things that's been an issue for me with all the other groups that I attend is time. I am practicing law, so it's impossible for me to be out developing my business and practicing law at the same time. One of the great things about NIA® is we only have to get together for our meetings once a month. It's less time consuming, and I still get the same results, if not more, by being part of NIA® than I did from the other groups I was involved with. In fact, this is by far the group I've had the most success getting business from.*
>
> **Suzanne DuBose**
> **Attorney**
> **NIA® Houston Group**

Expanded Networking Opportunities

I'm not sure which has exits clearing faster—Sunday morning church services or an early-morning networking group! You better not be near the door at the end, or you risk getting run over before you're even out of the parking lot. When you're meeting before your workday starts, you are going to be in a hurry to get out of there and start checking things off your to-do list. If you're a business owner, you may have already missed a number of important calls just during breakfast.

> **"I love the mini-meets!"**
>
> *I loved the mini-meet today! It was great to see those who were there. NIA®'s mini-meets are often more well-attended than my other networking group's mandatory meetings.*
>
> **Scott Adelman**
> **Adelman Insurance Services**
> **NIA® Katy Connectors**

This is one reason why we don't hold early-morning meetings. Though our franchise contract allows franchise leaders to hold meetings when they like, we encourage all of our franchise owners to hold them in the afternoon. Today, 100 percent of the ninety-minute NIA® meetings are in fact being held between 3:00-5:00 p.m. in cities across the country. The impact of an afternoon meeting is that members are able to stay and visit with each other when it's over.

> **"The fastest ninety minutes every month"**
>
> *The meetings are the fastest ninety minutes every month and give us ample time to network. I'm feeling cool.*
>
> **Tammy Schroder**
> **Veritas Title Partners**
> **NIA® Woodlands Group**

By holding meetings in the afternoon, usually at the end of the work day, you have the time to visit. You can set up one-on-ones with other members in your group, ask more questions about a referral someone gave you, or just get to know members better in a relaxed atmosphere. You have the time to build relationships, which is ultimately what networking is all about. This means that you have the opportunity to come and more completely do what you came to do.

Building Relationships That Last a Lifetime

You see, in many ways, networking is like a big sandwich. The middle of the sandwich is important, but it wouldn't be very good without something holding it together. People and relationships are what is holding your networking success in place. Even though we only have one mandatory meeting each month, we consistently provide other and more personal networking opportunities for our group members each month. We host happy hours, group events, educational lunch series, and more. We offer a variety of avenues for you to form deep relationships with your fellow group members because, again, *this is the most important part of networking.*

So, what if you actually *like* those early morning meetings? Well, go find one! Then, come see us in the afternoon. If you're already in a group you love, then stay—and let us add to the power of your network. You don't have to choose one or the other, and our model gives you time to do both, and to do them well.

At NIA®, we always put our members over our brand, and we actually encourage you to join other networking groups. Our first

> **"Meeting monthly lets me put more time into my business"**
>
> *I attend several networking meetings every month through various organizations, but NIA® is one of my favorites for a few reasons.*
>
> First, I love how efficient NIA® is, as we are only obligated to meet once a month.
>
> Second, they offer other networking opportunities during the month that have proven beneficial as well. In addition, not meeting weekly has saved me over eighty hours annually and lets me put more time into my business.
>
> Third, this leaves me ample time to visit with other members for one-to-ones as well as work in other networking opportunities. The Network In Action meetings are designed so that I get to know the business owners professionally as well as personally. Though we only meet once a month, the relationships I have formed here are every bit as solid as those from my weekly networking groups. I believe in the power of networking, as I have seen it work time and time again.
>
> **Natalie Coyle**
> **Shooting Star Promotions, Owner**
> **NIA® Heights Group**

priority is supporting your business growth, and we obviously believe that networking has the power to do that. So, go network! Have you ever met any business owners who got all of the business they need out of just one networking group? If you are currently only using one avenue for your own networking efforts, then you are reaching only a fraction of the people who are waiting to help you. However, if you're going to pick one avenue of networking, I humbly submit that you are likely to find the most qualified referrals in your local NIA® group.

Higher-Quality Members

By holding meetings once a month, we are finding that more and more business *owners* are signing up and taking the time to attend—whereas weekly meetings tend to attract the employees and sales representatives. The truth of the matter is that if you ask business owners whether they have an extra one hundred hours they can block out of their calendar over the next twelve months, they are going to look at you like you're crazy. However, we all know the importance of networking, so typically owners will send their sales person in their place. But who would *you* rather network with? When you set up a one-to-one, you want to make sure you're sitting across from the person who has the authority to write you a check and, better yet, has the power to refer you.

> **"The majority of members are business owners"**
>
> Network In Action is for experienced professionals interested in networking. The majority of members are business owners with years of experience. I appreciate my group leader, Moose Rosenfeld, for his hands-on involvement in vetting potential members to ensure he is bringing in great referral partners.
>
> **Paula Marion**
> **Simple Operational Solutions, Owner**
> **NIA® Bellaire Group**

In addition, holding fewer meetings attracts and retains higher numbers than the average early-morning get together. The standard organized networking group averages fourteen members. We *require* our groups to be a minimum of twenty-five members, and many of our groups are maintaining long-term membership numbers of thirty-five or more. It's not hard to figure out why. It's just easier to book something into your regular schedule when it's not asking so much of you.

At NIA®, we like to think that we ask you for less and deliver more.

9
Technology

A friend of mine joined a local networking group in Houston a couple of years ago and was told he had to attend an orientation class before he would be allowed to become a member of the group. This particular friend is a seasoned business owner and accomplished networker. I promise you that he could teach all of us a thing or two about networking. However, he was told in no uncertain terms that it was important that he be introduced into The BNI® Way.

Reluctantly, he agreed to attend and, as often happens in this big old city, he found himself running ten minutes late due to traffic problems. He showed up outside a locked door. After much banging on the door, the moderator finally made his way over to my friend and told him very pointedly that "showing up late was not the BNI® way," and that he was going to have to return at another time. I cannot print here what his response was.

Fast forward two years, and he's sipping wine at home while he's watching the Network In Action tutorials from his phone—doing things The NIA® Way.

He has been a great contributor to his NIA® group for years.

In today's world where our on-demand, technology-driven culture has made its way into every industry, the lack of technology in the world of networking groups is mind boggling. It's ridiculous and unnecessary to require you to take a few hours out of your busy schedule to learn how to be a good, loyal Kool-Aid drinker of whatever networking group you just joined. Most weekly, early-morning meetings run by volunteers rely on little slips of pink paper to keep track of referrals—both for the accounting of referrals from the collective group and for you personally to send and receive referrals. If you don't happen to have one of those little slips of paper in your back pocket when you come across a referral for someone in your group, oh well! It's frustrating watching all of these reports being given based on those bits of paper. Can that possibly be accurate? What if you did happen to capture a referral, but the paper ended up in the wash? Or crumpled up at the bottom of your purse? Or left on a countertop somewhere? It's just not practical.

At NIA®, we recognize that there is a better way.

"NIA®'s technology is so advanced!"

I have always been blown away by how little technology there is in other groups. On more than one occasion, I would have the intention of passing a referral and not have the old pink, yellow, or white papers with me and invariably forget the opportunity.

At NIA®, as long as I have my phone I have all the members' contact info, video of their company, and ability to pass the referral immediately. I love the fact that when I am sent referrals, my new prospects receive a video of me introducing myself and my company before I even call them.

The monthly meeting notification and the scoreboard keep me up-to-date. I can look at the scoreboard anytime to see how I rate in terms activity in the group! I used to really be annoyed at every meeting having to give my elevator pitch and listen to twenty-plus minutes of others' every meeting. NIA®'s technology is so advanced, it not only gives us a chance to network during the meetings, but throughout the month as well. I love the meetings as well as the results I am getting as a realtor!

Holly Grajales
Walzel Properties, Realtor
NIA® Heights Group

We like to treat our members like adults. We encourage you to take our orientation from the comfort of your own home at your leisure with our e-learning platform. Though you may not have those pink slips with you all the time, today it is a sure bet you will have your smart phone handy.

We spent eight months developing our proprietary platform that synchronizes with your smart phone so that you can send and receive referrals instantly. As long as you have access to your phone or your computer, you're in business. In addition, this technology keeps a record of all of your activity within the group so that you can keep an eye on the value you are creating and the value you are receiving with your membership. We like to say that if Facebook and LinkedIn had a baby—it would look like our NIA® platform.

With a tap of the screen, you are able to monitor all the details of your activity and stay connected with the group at large. You can RSVP for group events such as monthly meetings or supplemental networking opportunities, message members individually, and create your own personal marketing campaign within the group.

> **"The technology is powerful"**
>
> *I have never recorded a video introduction to myself before. The technology that sends this to my prospect when I am sent their referral is so powerful. I love Network In Action's technology!*
>
> **Arlis Steel**
> **Sienna Plantation**
> **NIA® Missouri City Group**

Our app gives you instant access to all of the following:

- **Pass a Referral**: When you hit the "pass" button and add the prospect's info, three things happen: First, you receive fifty points on the member scoreboard. Everyone in the group can see business is being transacted, which also reminds them to pass referrals as well. Second, the member receives the prospect's information in real time so he or she can reach out and capture that business. Third, the prospect receives an introduction to the member or referral recipient with both a short bio video and a link to the member's website. This is one of our most unique and popular features. It's no surprise that our members find this platform to be so much easier than the old tried-and-true, tri-colored paper of years past.

- **My Referrals**: This is where you will have constant access to the referrals that have been sent to you. The group leader also uses this feature to check to ensure our members are getting the referrals promised when they signed on. With this function, you never have to worry about losing a valuable prospect's contact information.

- **Sent Referrals**: This is similar to My Referrals, but in reverse. This is where you can view and keep track of all the referrals you have sent to other members. This data allows the group leader to easily monitor each member's commitment to pass referrals to existing members. If existing members are not doing their part, the franchise owners have that information right at their fingertips and can take appropriate action, which is always with the intention of making NIA® the most powerful and efficient networking option out there for business owners.

> **"I joined NIA® because of their technology"**
>
> *One of the reasons I joined Network In Action was because of their technology. You can go in and send and receive referrals in real time. You can link your other social media efforts, like your LinkedIn and Facebook Fan pages, straight to your other group members so that when you post, you are keeping the members up to date and you are staying front of mind. It's a great advantage and just one of the ways we utilize technology to keep from having to meet every single week. The technology really impressed me, and then you add the quality of business owners in the group. It's a great group of people, and the meetings are always fun and full of movement and action.*
>
> **Shannon Kmiec**
> **WorldPay, Owner**
> **NIA® Houston Group**

- **Pavement Points**: This is where you will monitor your involvement in the group. The more engaged you are, the greater your success and ROI will be. Pavement Points help track the number of physical meetings you attend as well as the extracurricular things, such as one-to-one meetings with other group members, tag-alongs, individual coaching sessions with the group leader, attending the monthly coaching session, or showing up for any other supplemental networking event such as a happy hour mixer. The points speak straight to the member scoreboard, which keeps track of everyone's activity.

- **Group Scoreboard**: This may be one of the NIA® team's best ideas. This is where you can see everyone's point totals. These points speak volumes. With a quick look, all members can see who the movers and shakers are in the group. Our NIA® members agree that by having the scoreboard, there is simply zero reason to bore everyone at meetings with twenty-five to thirty minutes of everyone standing up and reporting whether they have been good little boys or girls and passed a referral. At most NIA® meetings, less than five minutes are spent on this activity because we understand that today's business owner is simply looking for efficiency, including in their networking. Typically, a franchise owner will show a quick glimpse of the scoreboard and acknowledge the members who achieved the most since the last meeting. Guess what? This now leaves an additional twenty-five to thirty minutes to do what? Network! You know—what you came to do in the first place.

- **Create Connection**: This is one of the favorite tools of our NIA® management team. The idea was borne out of the fact that in traditional networking groups, once the group has finished passing around the low-lying fruit, the return for members starts to diminish. It is almost imperative that people are either asked to leave or replaced to make room for "new blood." At NIA®, we recognize that the referrals from mature business connectors are not just from the people in the room, but rather from the incredible group of people they know. These are secondary referrals. For instance, maybe you don't know anyone who is looking to buy a house, but you know a mortgage lender you can connect with the realtor in your group. Or, perhaps the pest control guy is looking to hire a new admin, and you know someone who you think would be a good fit. Connections include anyone who you feel can help to fill a need or support any of your group members in any way.

When you want to create a connection between someone in your group and someone in your circle of friends, all you have to do is tap on the app and click on the member's name and add your acquaintance's contact info. A single email then goes out immediately to both parties on your behalf that lets them know that, in your opinion, they can benefit from each other's acquaintance. Because both parties know you and trust you, they are likely to take action on this introduction. "Creating a Connection" immediately brings together the hundreds of people on your LinkedIn account and the thousands of other contacts you have—right at your fingertips. This is simply a better way to keep the group vibrant and active long after you have introduced yourself to other group members and given them obvious referrals.

- **Group Roster**: This is simply a quick reference of all the members in your group. If you are sitting at a railroad crossing and need a quick reminder of who's who, it is simply a click away. All members are listed alphabetically with their accompanying photo, video bio, and a link to their personal website. It gives you all the information you need to refer with confidence.

> **"NIA®'s technology keeps us all connected"**
>
> *It is amazing how NIA®'s technology keeps us all connected.*
>
> **Robert Trembath**
> **Spectrum 360 Technology Group**
> **NIA® Cyfair Connectors Group**

- **The NIA® Marketplace**: This is our latest technology advancement. We realized that as NIA® began to grow across the country, there were members who may have special skills to offer other members. Since existing NIA® members love referring people who they can trust, we wanted to expand their network across all of our groups across the country. We've done this by creating a marketing platform where you can post your special offers, and they are immediately accessible to the entire NIA® membership of hundreds of group members. In addition, when you need something for your business, you can log in and see if anyone is offering a special promotion on the exact services or products you're looking for. For example, let's say we have a patent attorney in one of our California groups, and a member in South Carolina needs patent work done. The NIA® marketplace creates a platform for these members to be able to find each other from across the entire country.

NIA® will always be about the spirit of giving, but our second highest calling is to keep business in the family. In today's global economy, we are able to help members anywhere a NIA® franchise is operating. With your help and the help of our advanced technology, we expect that reach to extend to fifty-one states and territories across the US and numerous countries around the globe within the next few years.

10
Refer With Confidence

When you give a referral to your friends, family members, or other contacts, you are taking responsibility, at least in some measure, for the outcome. The idea is that those who trust you will also trust your referral. By extension, you carry some of the responsibility for the quality of the work of the person you refer.

But how can you be sure that you are lending your trust to someone who deserves it? If, God forbid, you pass a referral and there is a criminal element involved, that reflects poorly on *you*. In most organized networking models, there are zero checks and balances when it comes to the character or background of the people who are enrolling. Your business isn't required to have five-star reviews in order for you to join. You aren't personally required to have a clean criminal record. You aren't vetted in any other way besides your ability to write a check. Sure, meeting with them regularly gives you a sense of comfort and familiarity, but you don't *really* know what that person's background looks like. So, how can you be sure that you are referring people who will protect your reputation as well as theirs?

At Network In Action, we make sure that you can always refer with confidence. Many companies join our networking groups for that reason alone. Recently, one new member, a CPA, commented that, "By joining NIA®, I will have quality companies to refer my customers to that I can trust." She was confident in that statement because we vet all prospective members before they are allowed to join. Each member has successfully passed a criminal background check and undergone a personality profile test. The criminal background check looks at anything that might have happened that would reflect poorly on you or the NIA® community. This means you can trust that when you refer anyone in NIA® to one of your personal contacts you have some security in who is doing the work.

In the early days of NIA®, I had an experience where I drove out to an appointment with our franchise owner west of Houston. When I got there a few minutes late, I saw they'd left a note on the door for me to join them at a restaurant just down the street. Once I arrived, I was uncomfortable in that small booth space talking to the prospective member—an attorney—about NIA® while he was already enjoying his big burger. The longer I stayed, the more uncomfortable I became. There was something about this guy's intensity and demeanor that was off-putting and cold. He stared at me with eyes that looked more like they belonged to an addict than an attorney.

> **"I *know* that it's a good referral"**
>
> *There are a lot of things I like about Network In Action, but the one thing I love the most is that when I get or give referrals, I know that they have had a personality assessment and a background check. That means when I refer someone or do business with a member of my group, I know that it's a good referral.*
>
> **Judy Maldonado**
> **American Southwest**
> **Mortgage Corp**
> **NIA® Heights Group**

As soon as I finished talking to him about NIA®, he immediately wanted to join. Our new franchise owner was eager to add a member, and I didn't have the heart to turn him down based on my own gut feelings. We signed him up, had him fill out the personality profile, and ran his background check. He scored extremely low on the personality profile, and as if that weren't enough, there was one small issue when we received the background report back at corporate: a conviction for manslaughter!

When I called the guy to tell him he would not be allowed into the group, he took it completely in stride. We were just grateful that our policies had allowed us to collectively dodge a bullet. My initial impression was right about that guy. Even though he was willing and able to write a check, he was no fit for NIA®. However, as of the writing of this book, he is an active member of another networking group in his community!

The point is, who you refer matters. Do you think anyone in this lawyer's current group would feel comfortable referring him to their personal contacts if they were privy to the information on his record? I can assure you they would not. At NIA®, that's simply not a concern.

In the history of NIA®, every member has been sent the personality profile and completed the background check, and no one has been accepted into our membership without this screening being done. We now have hundreds of members who are all daily referring their personal contacts to other members they know they can trust.

The Personality Profile

Before we approve your membership application for NIA®, we need to make sure that we are a good fit for each other. Your personality profile will reveal a bit about you and the way you value others. If you aren't interested in forming relationships with the people you're doing business with and business for, then we don't want to waste your time. We have built our entire model around relationships. We are not in the business of transactions. We are in the business of people. At the end of the day, we live by our mantra: "Network In Action—helping people build relationships that last a lifetime."

This is one of the main reasons we teach our franchise owners to never chase people. We recognize that if you have to chase someone now, the reality is that you will likely have to continue to chase that person once that individual is in the group. We don't want our leaders to stuff their groups full of warm bodies for the sake of numbers. We make sure they are committed to building out groups of committed people. That is the best way to ensure the health and success of each collective group as well as the individual members themselves.

Refer With Confidence

One of the greatest joys I have is going out with new franchise owners who are obviously eager and excited to build up their groups. Early on, they may have only three or four members, but then I see them meet with someone and, after the interview, they walk outside and say, "You know, I just don't think I want that person in my group." That's when I know that we have trained them properly. It's not about getting the transaction—it's about enrolling the type of people who are committed to building relationships.

I had an appointment with a business owner and potential member, and as we sat down to talk, I just didn't feel comfortable with him. He just seemed "slippery". When we got to the end of the discussion and talked about our guaranteed ROI, he said he wanted thirty audiovisual jobs, "And I don't hang TVs." As we closed up the meeting, I walked back to my car thinking, *Well, you're not going to hang anything for Network In Action members because you're not a fit for this group.*

> **"I *know* that my reputation is in good hands"**
>
> *One of the crazier notions in networking is that as soon as people pay their fee, the entire membership is expected to start referring them without even knowing them. Though this is the case with all of the other networking groups, it is not with NIA®. The required background check gives me confidence that I can refer all members and know that my reputation is in good hands. The personality profile helps to bring together givers, and that inspires me to see how many of the members I can help first, knowing that they, too, are looking out for me.*
>
> **Rich Iazzetti**
> **Handyman**
> **NIA® Franchise Owner**
> **NIA® Cyfair Group**

We look for people who have reasonable expectations for their results and who ask questions like, "Who are the other members of the group? Tell me about the makeup of your membership. I want to make sure I can be a help to them and refer other people to them."

Our personality profile goes a long way in identifying those characteristics in people. It helps us build out a group of business owners who recognize the importance of focusing first on the needs of the other members. In this way, we are able to strategically create a group of givers who will over-deliver for any of the contacts you refer to them. This increases the likelihood that every job will be performed to the client's satisfaction.

Relationships, Relationships, Relationships

In addition, our platform is geared toward creating actual relationships with other group members. As you take the time to form meaningful relationships with each member in your group, you will be able to do more than just pass along a phone number. When you refer a member from any industry, you'll be able to honestly say, "This is a good guy. You'll like him," or "This is a trustworthy woman. She will bring integrity to your project." You can say that with confidence because you can trust that the franchise owners have done their job and properly vetted the member.

These kinds of details make a difference, especially in our culture. They create an immediate emotional connection, which makes your prospect more likely to call. Research shows that people make decisions about whether to buy with their emotions first, and then use logic to justify the decision they've already made.

This is not only applicable to the referral or referee scenario. It is applicable to your relationships with the people you refer as well. If other members sincerely know and like you, your name and company are going to come to their minds much more readily when it's time to pass it along. Your fellow group members will be able to refer you as confidently as you are able to refer them.

11
Building Your Community Through Service

At a Network In Action meeting North of Houston in the Woodlands, there are small groups of people scattered around the room busily discussing what charities and local service projects they want to get behind. During the discussion, it comes out that two of its group members have children with juvenile diabetes. One of those members volunteered just a few days before to head up this year's Juvenile Diabetes Gala. The night he agreed to do that, he lay in bed with his eyes wide open, wondering where he was possibly ever going to get all the volunteers he needed to pull off that gala. However, when the NIA® group hears that two of its members have children with this disease, the entire group volunteers to work the gala in the fall. His problem of recruiting volunteers is over!

The gala ends up being a success, and today, that group is still heavily involved with raising money and participating in this annual event.

This emphasis on service and giving back is at the core of who we are as a company. It's not separate from our culture—it *is* our culture. As we continue to grow the company and continue to make this a requirement, we want this to be our hallmark.

My last business was very lucrative, easily bringing in seven figures annually for a number of years. I always talked about creating a foundation, but never did it. It's one of the great regrets of my life. We didn't start where I felt we needed to first—which is to be socially responsible and conscious of those who aren't as blessed as we might be. I decided when we started NIA® that we would not make that

> **"You are helping us find a cure for Type 1 diabetes!"**
>
> *Scott, thank you very much for your very generous donation through Stacy's NIA® Team Builders to JDRF. You are helping us find a cure for Type 1 diabetes. We so greatly appreciate your support and that of our entire NIA® group. You are awesome! Thank you! Thank you! Thank you!*
>
> **Drew, Patty, and Phillip Wilkerson
> Beacon Enterprises
> The Woodlands Group**

mistake again. With NIA®, we put first things first. We decided from day one that every one of our franchises would participate in some kind of community outreach project each year in order to give back to the communities that have been so good to us.

Therefore, when we sit down with prospective franchise owners, one of the things we always ask is, "What are you doing charitably?" We ask that question prior to the disclosure that heading up these projects is going to be one of their responsibilities as an owner. We want to make sure the seeds of that service are already there. It's at the core of NIA®, how we choose our leaders, and how we choose our group members.

This makes perfect sense because if you think about great networkers, they're the people with the biggest hearts. They're the people who are always looking out for others. If you take a group of these successful, professional, and powerful people, they all have gifts to bring to the table and are willing to bring them. Our call to our members is this: We want you to bring your gift. Some years, that may be your talent; some years, that may be your time; some years, that may be your money. We never want you to give to the point of hardship, but we encourage everyone in the group to bring *something*.

How it Works

At some point each year, your group will break out into smaller groups, each representing a different area of interest. The members move to the group where their hearts move them to. Some members may be interested in helping the environment, some may want to serve victims of abuse, and others may want to help veterans, or pets, or any number of great causes. These small groups have a short discussion in which all of the members are allowed the opportunity to articulate which philanthropic efforts they are passionate about. Then each small group comes to an agreement on exactly which cause they want to take on and how to execute the service project before electing a spokesperson, who then stands up in front of the entire meeting and tries to sell everyone else on their concept of who or what they want to support.

Ultimately, each NIA® group comes up with a project that its entire membership is going to get behind. Each project is typically an ongoing endeavor of three to five months. It may be something as simple as going to the food bank for two or three hours on a Saturday, where members will have time to network while also giving back to a great organization. Or, it could be something as big as a festival for veterans.

The VetFest

We first launched this idea in the eleventh month of our first group, the NIA® Houston Heights Group. I am announcing this initiative and wondering where it will lead. I have a great amount of trepidation, as this is our first introduction of this big idea for every NIA® member in every group to give something back. As the group breaks up into smaller groups, some members go to a table to discuss how to cut down on sex trafficking since the NFL's Super Bowl is coming to town in a few months, and this problem seems to travel annually to the host city. Other members discuss child abuse, the environment, and pet adoption. Then there is one table that is getting particularly loud and passionate about veterans when suddenly, this crazy guy, Tyler Peck, the owner of The Spaghetti Western Italian Café, stands up and says, "We need to do a VetFest! We need to do it on Veteran's Day and have beer and food! We will have bands,

> **"NIA® gives back to the community"**
>
> *NIA® is the only networking group I know of that actually gives back to the community. I'm very grateful to be a part of this. Thanks!*
>
> **Sean McCoy
> Charity Corps
> NIA® Sienna Plantation Group**

Building Relationships That Last a Lifetime

and booths for kid, and we can start in the parking lot in the afternoon and end late at night!" I'm standing there thinking, *Slow down, cowboy, how are we ever going to pull this off in three months?* I am also thinking that perhaps I need to be more careful about what I ask for, as I am looking ahead and seeing how this could get really out of hand!

Ultimately, the group elects a chair person, retired soldier Ms. Maureen Roberts with Cardinal Delivery in Houston, Texas, and she teams up with forty-one other business owners from two NIA® groups to put together VetFest 2016. They research different charities and finally select a charity called "Combined Arms" to work with, which is a brilliant organization. As we learned from Combined Arms, on average, veterans take four to six years to integrate back into society when they leave the military. Their populations are rife with divorces, people who lose houses, those who have PTSD, and those who are really struggling to get back on their feet in a number of ways. Yet, these are really talented people who still have a lot to offer their communities and deserve the best of jobs after serving their country. They just don't know where to go. When soldiers come to Combined Arms, this charity does an assessment to see what the soldiers need, and then they pair them with one or more of the twenty-six different charities they're working with, all under one roof.

> **"Great organizations look to give back. NIA® is a great organization."**
>
> *I joined NIA® to help grow my delivery service. Before I knew it, I volunteered to chair the first-ever VetFest sponsored by several NIA® groups. Not only was the experience personally rewarding, I connected with more business owners in a deeper, more meaningful way.*
>
> *I think it is really cool that at NIA®'s core, it wants to be an organization that gives back to the communities we are in. Great organizations look to give back. NIA® is a great organization.*
>
> **Maureen Roberts**
> **Cardinal Delivery Service**
> **NIA® Cypress Group**

Over the course of the next three months, we see all kinds of different businesses come together—one donates the branding, another the website, one company contributes the SEO for the event, and others contribute the bands, T-shirts for sale, volunteers to build the stage, and everything else we need in order to pull off a successful event. It is a huge success, and everyone involved really bonds and connects with each other. Crowds of veterans come out and attend, and it is a very moving day all around.

We end up spending a grand total of $126 on the entire event and raising over $8,000! It's enough money to turn a naked conference room into a powerful, multi-use training center for veterans. It's a place they can go to be trained on how to write resumes, take classes on improving their credit or saving their mortgage, and more. The room is equipped with technology to support all of these endeavors. In fact, the audio-visual company involved ended up only charging their costs for the project. They are one of many companies who gave their ideas, money, or time.

Giving and Getting Back

Fast forward a year after our dear Maureen volunteered to lead us on VetFest, and she received the shattering news that she has been diagnosed with lung cancer. The group that worked with her most closely voted that this year's charity would involve one thing and one thing only: assisting Maureen as much as possible. They're providing transportation to treatments when needed and a maid service for her home twice a month so that when she's there she can be comfortable.

Her story shows the true beauty of this truth: When we give, no matter how much we think we are giving, we always get back more in return. That's what we want NIA®, at its core, to be about. At the end of the day, NIA® is about taking action—action to grow our businesses and to serve our communities that have been so good to us. We have sixteen different charitable projects going on in Houston right now, and that number continues to rise in cities across the US as we add more and more franchises across the country.

More Than I Dreamed

This service model surpasses my dream of starting a foundation. If we'd started a foundation, we would have only been raising money and helping maybe one or two select causes. Originally, we thought that perhaps we should keep our service efforts close to the brand—for instance, maybe we should focus on teaching entrepreneurs at the colleges or mentoring kids. But then I thought, *You know what? Every single one of our groups are full of people who already have causes close to their heart. Let's let them choose.*

Our current model is so far beyond anything I could have dreamed in my last business. We're attracting people who *want* to participate and who have the means to do so, even if they aren't able to write a check, because they have such incredible and diverse talents they are ready and willing to share. Our members are bringing gifts from their hearts to the

---

"A very happy ending, and a great example of the power of networking!"

In the aftermath of Hurricane Harvey that hit Houston, one of our members was volunteering at one of the relief centers where she was handing out food, cleaning supplies, and clothing. One of the greatest needs was help with getting cleaning supplies out to the neighborhoods that had been hardest hit so that they could start to clean out and rebuild. A factory in Keene, Texas, had offered eight thousand industrial-size buckets to the relief center so that the buckets could be filled with cleaning supplies at the relief center and then distributed to the survivors. The problem was that Keene is three and a half hours away from Houston, and that was a lot *of buckets that needed to be transported.*

My member who was volunteering put out a plea on Facebook for help in getting the buckets from point A to point B. I saw the post, called her right away, and told her about another member we have in another NIA® group who is VP of a logistical trucking company. She made the call, told him the situation, and a couple hours later, problem solved! Not only did the trucking company make a seven-hour drive to pick up and deliver the buckets, but it did it absolutely free*! This was a very happy ending and a great example of the power of networking.*

Stacy Harris
NIA® Franchise Owner of Four Groups
NIA® The Woodlands Groups

communities they already love, and which have loved them back. NIA® is helping build relationships that last a lifetime!

12
Be a Value Creator

You have people who mistakenly come into a group who think that the concept of networking is that you go into a group and say, "Hey, open up your Rolodex and show it to me, and I will pick who I want out of there in order to get new business." I call that the popcorn mentality—the idea that it's going to happen fast and be a simple two-step process. You join and BAM! You have a new list of leads to call.

That's the opposite of networking, which is very much the art of developing relationships. The old adage that anything worth working for takes time and commitment is true. Once people trust you, they will open up their heart and introduce you to the people they know who can help you. It has been said that networking is more like the law of the farm. You have to plant your seed, nurture it, and wait for the harvest.

Seasoned and skillful networkers understand this. They know that if they show up in a sell-only mode, they will alienate themselves from the rest of the group. It is counterproductive. I often see guests and novice networkers who just want to come to the group and sell. They might as well have a scarlet letter on their chest because in short order, the real networkers in the group will avoid them like the plague. In networking meetings, these types earn a reputation. Members see them coming and quickly find someone else to engage with.

If you have a sales-first mentality, you are forgetting the first premise of networking. Not only are you going to offend a lot of people, you're never going to have the opportunity to cross the initial barrier of trust and gain access to referrals. If people don't feel important to you beyond the sale, they certainly aren't going to send people they love and respect your way to get the same treatment. You really have to be cognizant of the fact that you're going to a networking environment first and foremost to build relationships.

Owners vs. Employees

Business owners seem to better understand the fact that when you build relationships, multiple sales will follow. They understand that this takes time. One of the accidental consequences of Network In Action's model of holding monthly instead of weekly meetings is that we have more business owners in our group than sales people. This means we are able to assemble groups of people who understand these principles from the get go.

> **"I quit networking until I found NIA®"**
>
> *I started networking over twenty years ago. I quit because it just wasn't giving me results anymore. When I found NIA®, I decided to give it another try because I only have to go once a month.*
>
> **Konrad Orzechowski**
> **Kay Plumbing Services, Owner**
> **NIA® Capitol Columbia Group**

In addition, there's no pressure on the business owners to run back to the office and say they got a sale. But if you're the sales person in the group, you're typically there because the business owner doesn't want to attend a weekly meeting. You have to go back to the sales manager or the owner and tell him what you've done every week, and you want to be able to say you got a sale. The very nature of the weekly meeting creates an environment where there are more people there who are interested in selling than networking.

Let go of the popcorn mentality that you have to leave with a sale. Instead, keep the mentality that, no matter what happens, at the end of the day, you have amplified your reach and now have more people who are able to talk about your business with others than you ever have before in your life.

For some people, this understanding comes easily. For others, they just can't get there. And if you can't get there, you are not going to find networking to be an effective way to grow your business or bring meaningful business to others. This will lead you to find fault with and criticize the leader, the model, the industry, and everyone in the group when, in reality, you didn't go there with the right purpose in the first place.

Come to Serve

In order to be successful in networking, you must first understand what networking is really all about. It is about creating relationships, and the only way you're going to build a relationship is by positioning yourself as a giver who can be trusted. When you walk through the doors, let your biggest question be, "How can I create value for the people I meet?" When you start out with that giving attitude, you will naturally attract people to you. That is what lies at the heart of networking.

Even when you meet someone who is not a good fit for the product or service you offer, you can be thinking about who you know who is the best fit for the person you're talking to. When you are sincerely listening and sincerely care about the needs of others, you are positioned to help fill those needs in some way.

Fundamentally, at the end of the day, the biggest difference between NIA® and any other networking group is that our whole model is crafted to ensure we are adding value to our members and not meeting to impress the guests. We are meeting to serve *you*.

When you go to network, remember that you are there for a reason, which is to try and learn as much as you can about other people's businesses. For NIA® members, this includes their families, what they do on vacation, what drives them as business owners, and their personal challenges and victories. That is the kind of relationship that facilitates deep and meaningful connections. When you know and trust each other, you will refer to each other. That kind of depth requires you to be somewhat vulnerable and open. If that vulnerability doesn't come easily to you, or if you aren't a natural networker, you will have a period of time where you have to overcome a measure of discomfort to get there. It helps to be prepared with the right questions that will immediately show your readiness to connect and offer value.

Learn the Right Questions

When you meet people and ask them what they do, be prepared to ask a few follow-up questions, such as:

- Who is your ideal client?

- What needs are you currently looking to fill in your business?

- Who is your ideal contact, or who is already working with the kind of people who are your ideal clients?

Not only are these questions going to better position you to find qualified referrals for the people you're connecting with, but your sincerity and genuine interest in serving them will open the door to a reciprocal relationship.

It is also important to learn the right questions to ask your friends and family members to see where you can help fill their needs with your extensive network. One of the things we do in our meetings pretty early on—and the reason we do it is to help everyone in the group to understand the value every single member brings—is an exercise in which you leave the meeting, not with a sale, but with three qualifying questions from every member and business in the group that you can ask your friends. If you know the questions to ask, then the answers will help you dictate who to refer to. In addition, you are able to better meet the needs of your friends and families by leading them to the people who can help them with their relevant and timely needs.

Qualifying questions may include:

"Who are you currently using for your pest control?"

"When was the last time you checked to see if you are getting the most affordable car insurance?"

"Have you had your HVAC serviced lately? It's important to do that before the change in seasons."

"What's one habit you feel is keeping you from allowing you to be as successful as possible?"

"Do you feel like your team members are working as efficiently as possible and are committed to your company's objectives?"

As you can see, these questions are aimed at revealing the real needs of the people who are already in your life. When you are able to connect the two parties, you have served everyone. These questions are powerful tools in creating more value in all of your relationships and are on each one of our members' profiles on our website. This is also true for you. When you share your own qualifying questions on your profile, the other members are able to become spokespeople for you as well.

One of the reasons we can do this is because, again, our technology provides us with *time* in the meetings to network.

Master the One-to-One

It is equally important to ensure that you are creating value during your one-to-ones. We encourage our members to get to know each other outside of the networking meetings in a more personal atmosphere. I can honestly say that I have never been to a one-to-one meeting with a member where I did not walk away from that time having learned something valuable about that person or that person's business. Most often, besides the time spent bonding and cementing the relationship, I will come away with some new piece of information about that person's business that I was previously unaware of. Rarely do these short get togethers not pay an immediate dividend, and they always get me closer to that individual, which creates a stronger desire to help that person and the person's business.

Making the Change

At NIA®, we welcome the seasoned networkers as well as those who are excited to learn a better way.

For many people, this value-driven mentality can't be taught. This is why we have such a rigorous screening procedure in our application process. However, for others, it's a matter of shifting a few core attitudes, which opens up your entire world.

I, along with so many other business owners, have been grateful to realize the truth—that not only you can be successful in business by sincerely and authentically treating people as you wish to be treated, but, even more important, *it is the only way* networking truly works!

13
Networking Dos and Don'ts

Robert Kiyosaki, the author of *Rich Dad, Poor Dad*, said, "The richest people in the world look for and build networks. Everyone else looks for work."

The value of creating and maintaining your personal network can completely transform your business. However, there is an art to it, and if you're doing it wrong, you're lucky if the only consequence is no business as a result! In the typical networking meetings out there, you may be able to get by even if all you do is sit back and watch because the meetings are designed around the guests. You can go to most traditional networking groups and sit there very passively with an attitude and still get some value out of it. (However, most weekly networking meetings leave little time to truly network.)

To become a master networker, however, you need to adopt the best networking practices. This takes mindfulness and intention. You will be most successful when you take time to prepare yourself for each networking meeting you attend. If you were going into a meeting with someone who is building your website, you would be prepared. You would be focused and know the purpose of that meeting before you ever walked through the door. That is the same way you should treat any networking meeting. Be prepared by knowing what to do and what not to do. Here are some of the basics:

Show Up – Mentally and Physically

Showing up physically is important for obvious reasons. If you're not there, you're not networking, which is a sure way to ensure that networking isn't going to work for you. So, first and foremost—be there!

People join networking groups and sabotage themselves all the time by thinking they just have to sign the check and walk through the door. This couldn't be further from the truth.

When you take the time to be there in person, make sure you're also showing up with your attitude, heart, and mind. I have seen people come into other meetings and sit down in the corner and pull out their laptops and start doing work instead of mingling. As previously stated, networking is like a sandwich—what goes on before and after the meeting is just as important as what happens in between. So, if you're there working on your computer, what are you saying to your fellow members while they're walking around getting to know each other? You're screaming at them that you're socially uncomfortable, your work is more important than theirs, or that you just don't care about learning more about them. So why *would* they want to refer to you? These are all great ways to keep members from getting comfortable with you.

Put away the distractions and be present.

We do our best to create an environment that will help you do that. We know 100 percent of the people in our meetings have cell phones, so after checking in on Facebook at the beginning of the meeting, giving yourself pavement points for attending, and putting your next Network In Action meeting and any coaching sessions you have coming up onto your calendar, the franchise owner requires everyone to put their cell phones away. It's just too tempting to be distracted when you have your office right at your fingertips.

In many of our groups, the group leaders have instituted a rule that if someone is on a cell phone at all during the meeting, then that person has to buy someone else in the group a drink at the end of the meeting. Whatever the rules are from group to group, at the end of the day, we're creating an environment where people want to be there, and they are committed to making the other people in the room the most important thing for the next ninety minutes.

Send a Sub

When you can't be there in person, it's important that you send a substitute. We understand that things come up—an opportunity for a big sale, client fires, or a personal matter that requires immediate attention. That's going to happen to you, as it happens to the best of us. However, *when* it happens, send someone to attend in your place.

If four people are getting together for a campout and they each agree to bring one of the four meals that weekend, what happens when only three people bring food? The whole group is going to have to skip a meal, and you can bet there is going to be some animosity towards the person who didn't bring his share. It's the same thing with networking. If thirty people show up when they all could have been doing something "more important," and yet they still make the sacrifice to come, and you don't, what you're screaming at them is, "My time is more important than yours." That's the last thing you want people to feel when you're trying to build trust.

People often don't realize how important it is to send a substitute. However, those who value networking and value relationships will take the time to find one. And honestly, finding substitutes for an NIA® meeting is not nearly as painful to find as it would be for those traditional meetings. At our meetings, they are going to be treated to real networking, a beer or wine, a nice appetizer, and the meetings are full of great business owners and decision makers.

Check Your Mood at the Door

Be sure to check your mood at the door. There's no one in the group who is going to listen to you go on and on about the drama in your life and then feel comfortable referring to you. If you show up and only want to talk about your children's problems and how they're taking you away from work, or how you can't focus because you're getting a divorce, or how you're taking care of a sick family member and you're taking time off to deal with that—why would anyone want to refer someone to you? And yet, people do just this all the time.

We had a member a couple years ago who represented a local dental office. She came to every meeting and bashed her employer the entire ninety minutes. After two or three meetings of this, I finally pulled her to the side and said, "Do you think there is anyone in this room who wants to send their family members or friends to your office for dental work when you're bashing all of its business principles and questioning its integrity? Nobody's going to refer to you. You're wasting your time." After another month or two of the same type of attitude, we replaced her.

Bringing drama into a meeting does not give people confidence to refer to you. It's not a place to go to dump your problems and your attitudes on the other members. They're there to learn about your business—and *you*. If you want others to refer to you, refrain from airing all of your or your company's dirty laundry. Treat the opportunity professionally and check your drama at the door.

Avoid Cliques

Most networking groups are full of cliques, though that is the last thing you want when you're paying to connect with all the members. This isn't just true for those who may be left out of cliques—this is also true for the "in crowd." Each member in your group comes with unique gifts to offer. Don't limit your association to just a few select members, or you will miss out.

You're not likely to see cliques in our groups, even if you have a tendency to move toward them. Our leadership is armed with strategies that guarantee you're not going to see a clique for more than one meeting. We train our franchise owners to be on the lookout for them. Because we move around in every meeting, we can move people who are in a clique to another spot to participate in another activity with other people. No one in the group even knows it's happening. However, one of the things that I'm told most often by guests is, "I've never been to a networking group where I was so welcomed and felt so little pressure to join." I'm often told by members, "You know, one of the things I love about Networking in Action is that there aren't any cliques."

Use Your Business Card Appropriately

The number-one mistake I see most often is people not carrying a business card, not having a card that appropriately represents their brand, or using the business card as a way to avoid making an adequate connection with other people.

Bringing business cards sounds so simple, but even I sometimes find that I didn't bring enough cards to an event. However, you absolutely need to have a professional business card that represents your brand. It amazes me when I meet people who understand the value of branding, spend large amounts of money to brand themselves, and then throw together a business card that's unprofessional, doesn't represent their brand, or don't even carry a card with them.

Others may have an appropriate business card, but they don't know how to use it. They immediately stick the business card in people's hands before they've even had the chance to make eye contact or some other form of emotional connection to get the person to remember them. Giving out a few business cards doesn't mean you're networking, nor does the number of cards you give out serve as an appropriate measure of whether or not you had a successful event. Yes, you want business cards. Yes, you want them to be professional. But you don't want to simply let the business cards do the talking for you.

Be Prepared

You need to have a focus prior to coming into the meeting. Just as you wouldn't walk into a sales call, a webinar, or any other presentation without being prepared, you shouldn't walk into a networking meeting without some kind of preparation either. Sometimes that's just as simple as looking in the mirror and having a meeting with "the board of directors" and deciding that you're going to make this the most valuable time of your week or month because it has the potential to increase your business.

Learning the Trade

Above all, be patient with yourself as you learn the trade of successful networking. Some people are natural networkers. They can walk into any room and they're comfortable. For other people, it doesn't come as easily. However, they can still be great networkers. At NIA®, we challenge you to come as an active participant, and we create avenues to help you do so more naturally. From the way that we arrange the room to the activities we choose, our aim is to help you successfully network, even if you're not already an accomplished networker. We gently put you in a position to naturally stimulate your networking skills.

To take full advantage of that opportunity, you need to come with your game face on and be ready to go.

14
To the Millennials

Now I need to have a not-so-private conversation with the millennials. First, Network In Action has a place for you, too. Second, this organization is going to stretch you a little bit, but in a good way. And finally, when you succeed here as a member of our group, you will be prepared to succeed in every other aspect of your life. So, I invite you to come, learn, and stay.

You are a master of this fast-paced culture where everything happens for you in an instant. You don't have to wait on food, mail, relationships, transportation, or information. Something this culture is not equipped to hand you in an instant, though, is a purpose. I know you crave that. I know you want to make an impact on the world around you. I know that you hunger to be seen and acknowledged for what you have to offer. I know that you want to contribute in a meaningful way. You are surrounded by people who tell you that you can be and achieve anything you want. However, what is often left out of that conversation is that in order for you to be and to get, you have to *do*. And it's not about taking a certain number of steps, it's about taking the right steps.

Relationships

We want to be at the forefront of teaching you, the next generation of business owners, about networking and the importance of sound business relationships. We coach you on how to build relationships that last a lifetime. In order for people to be comfortable referring to you, they have to know you, trust you, and know you're going to take care of their family and friends. As a referral, you are an extension of their reputation, and they're not going to put their hard-earned reputation at risk for a stranger they barely know. You can't build that kind of relationship of trust by glancing down at someone's name tag a few times a month. You can't do that over a cup of coffee at Starbucks. You can't do that when you're just waiting for people to stop talking about what they do so that you can tell them more about yourself. No. Meaningful relationships take time and consistent deposits into the relationship bank account.

This is why world leaders get together for extended periods of time. Things happen when you spend time with people. There's a long history of adversaries getting together because that one-on-one time opens you up to seeing things in a new way and with a new perspective. Leaders of the world go to Camp David to spend time together or they gather on the golf course because they understand that deals, alliances, and treaties don't come from strangers. They come from people they like and trust. They come from relationships. Regardless of where you are right now in your career, it can only be improved by coming to understand the importance of relationships.

Planting Seeds

I had a young guy join one of our Houston groups who worked for a telecommunications business. He was very socially forward and made friends fast. People warmed up to him and he warmed up to people easily. After being in the group about four months, he changed companies and wanted to drop out of NIA® because he didn't think it was a good fit for him anymore. He wanted to spend his time exclusively with owners of large companies who had "multiple phone lines and needed massive telecommunications needs." So, he was looking at the people in the room and saying, "These people can't help me."

I told him, "It works for every industry, but it doesn't work for every person." That means that every industry can benefit from networking, but not every person knows how to make that happen. He didn't understand that he wasn't there to get business from the pest control guy or to be hired by the CPA. He was there to gain access to the hundreds and thousands of people *they* knew within their churches, communities, families, and schools. This is a mistake that a lot of people make. They don't understand that these relationships are the doorway to the real harvest. He was only focusing on the low-hanging fruit. He also failed to realize how much he, personally, had to offer the group.

He couldn't be persuaded to stay, and we do not chase our members. You either get it, or you don't.

Within ten days of his leaving the group, I bumped into him. He mentioned to me that his wife had been out of work for over a year. He'd been struggling with his mortgage, his two car notes, and meeting the needs of his beautiful daughter. However, his wife had just gotten a new position that was introduced to her by a member of his NIA® networking group. Because of the relationship of trust he'd formed with another woman in the group, she had gone to bat for his wife and helped her find a job. Now, that's a heck of a return on investment! Even though he didn't give it enough time to reap the kind of customer he was looking for, those contacts were life-changing for his family.

There is no way to rush these types of relationships. You just have to keep showing up and showing up the right way. If you're not finding the success you hoped for, then you have to look in the mirror before you start pointing fingers at the group. These are proven strategies and techniques across thousands of individuals and every single industry on the planet. If something is off, it may be your approach that needs adjusting. If you are practicing the techniques, then trust that the time-honored tradition of building relationships will have a payday.

A Learning Opportunity

This is what networking is truly about. This is why we make it such a high priority to first set these expectations with our members and to teach them what true networking is all about. Most groups don't teach networking. Honestly, I can't think of a single other group that does. You just have to show up and perform the best you know how. At the end of the day, it's a game of survival of the fittest. You sink, or you swim. However, networking is not a game of luck. It is a game of strategy.

At NIA®, we will hand you the playbook for successful networking practices. Your group leader will work with you, one-on-one if necessary, to help you master the techniques that will bring you success.

This is not some vague concept of success, either. Your success in NIA® is first measured by the minimum ROI that you and your group leader have agreed you *must* have within your first year. That success is our guarantee.

We will teach you about the importance of relationships and the law of the farm. We will show you the ins and outs of successful networking so that you can easily grow your business and your network. It's imperative that you learn these skills—not just for your sake, but for ours. You are the next generation of leaders! There are nuances to leadership and relationships that you can't learn without being steeped in that culture. At NIA®, we want to be a part of your growth.

A Purpose

We also want to help you find your dream and your purpose. We will do that by first lending you ours. You will find that the best way to find yourself—your passion, your drive, your vision—is to first lose yourself in service. Your unique talents and passion for helping others will in turn help others who may be less fortunate.

We recognize the value of service, which is why we create service opportunities for all of our group members. Other networking groups don't have time or even an interest in community service because they are so absorbed in the volunteer labors of managing their groups. Community service isn't even on their radar. But with NIA®, this is the core of our culture—giving back to the communities that have been so good to us. It's about making an offering of our talents and gifts, while also understanding that what we put out there comes back to us a hundred-fold.

As we thoroughly discussed in *Chapter 11: Building Your Community Through Service*, every group is required to do an annual community service project. Every group has to find something to get behind in order to give back to their community. You will have an equal say within your group as you come up with ideas of what to do. The group members themselves are responsible for selecting their cause because we understand that you already have causes that are close to your heart.

The first gift we ask of you is that you share that cause with us and let us get behind it with you.

Come, Learn, Stay

The path to anything you want is worth the journey. You may be tempted to shy away from the journey and the waiting and move on to the low hanging fruit. But I'm here to promise you that if you stay on the higher path, there are just a finite number of steps you need to take to get you where you want to go.

You can know for certain whether we are a good fit for you by asking yourself these two questions: How many people do you know today who understand your business and the type of customers you need? How many of those people are committed to going out of their way to help you grow your business?

If that number is less than thirty, then you should look closely at joining an NIA® group.

As you come to NIA® and allow yourself to integrate into our culture, you will become a master at networking. This will set you apart from your peers. You—who understand how to apply the law of the farm and build meaningful, mutually profitable relationships in every area of your universe—will be in a better position than your competitors in business and in life.

To The Millennials

Made in the USA
Columbia, SC
21 July 2023